How to Stay Productive When the World Is Ending

How to Stay Productive When the World Is Ending

Productivity, Burnout, and Why Everyone Needs to Relax More Except You.

Reductress™

Andrews McMeel
PUBLISHING®

To our daddy, Elon Musk.

Introduction:

How to Do Nothing and Everything and Still Feel Guilty about Both

Were you talented and gifted as a child, but found that all that effort of getting into the right school or the right job hasn't paid off? Were you average as a child and experienced more or less the same? Have you found yourself working relentlessly, losing sleep and friends, such that your life is basically *The Devil Wears Prada* but not actually glamorous at all? Maybe you should quit working so hard and take a bath. Or maybe you need to work even harder until you burst straight through that glass ceiling and into space with the other billionaires? We're pretty sure those are your only two choices, and only one of them requires cleaning a bathtub—just saying!

Maybe you've found yourself stuck between these two competing narratives and feel like you can't seem to do either right. You're not alone—most people can't do anything right.[1] Everything that shapes our adult working world has us feeling inadequate, insecure, and wondering if anything our parents taught us about life (Will I be able to retire? Will there be a planet Earth in 2050? If I roll my eyes will they really get stuck like that?) will ever come true. With all these new worries, you may be constantly asking yourself, "What am I supposed to be doing with my life when the world may or may not be ending?" Don't worry—we're going to explore all the ways to answer this question, but also show you exactly how you can blame your parents and society because, honestly, it's all their fault.[2]

---

1   What sets us apart is how many years we'll spend apologizing.
2   They should have let the world end in Y2K like it was supposed to!

If someone had broken into your home to rob you of everything that brings you joy and you caught them, you'd grab a butcher's knife and yell, "Get out of my house!" before falling to the floor crying over how scary it was to have to hold a knife like that. But the current situation in America is more like if someone had been stealing twenty bucks out of your pocket[3] every few weeks over the course of your life: The work you do is definitely reaping fewer rewards than it used to, but you aren't totally positive that it's your fault. Maybe you should stop carrying loose $20 bills in your pocket, but that doesn't feel like the real solution to the problem. And if it happens over generations, then adages like "Hard work pays off!" slowly evolve from solid advice to something that is only sort of true in certain situations to an ancient myth from the elders that we have to bookend with, "It's a nice idea, but don't take it too literally; it was written thousands of years ago to ensure the masses would be scared into remaining active on Slack for twenty-four hours a day."

We're not saying this is a deliberate conspiracy of the billionaire class or anything; they're too busy hustling and grinding to do that kind of stuff.[4] But even before people posted photos of themselves with yachts and tigers on Instagram, our culture falsely equated success with true happiness. So how much time are you putting toward achieving "success," and how much time are you putting into being happy? Or do you have time for neither because you were simply trying to "pay the rent" but were accidentally "hit by an electric scooter" and your insurance has a "$5,000 deductible" and you are now in "significant debt"? Answers may vary!

In the year 1869, neurologist Dr. George Beard identified an illness called "neurasthenia," which was later coined in the 1970s as "burnout," and fifty years later, we may know it as "regular life." Although Dr. Beard was a white guy from Connecticut, he was one of the most prominent voices to warn that modern civilization is making humans straight up lose their minds, and for that, he is an ally. Dr. Beard called neurasthenia "a disorder of modernity, caused by the fast pace of urban life that puts excessive demands on people's brains"[5] and, like, how did he *know*? This feeling has become so normal that fixing it seems like one of those things that people talk about but never actually do—like saving for retirement or "drinking water."[6]

---

3 Even worse if it was a dress pocket; they were supposed to liberate us!

4 The very nice and hot billionaires did not pay us to say this!

5 The treatment for white women with neurasthenia was (sometimes forced) "rest cures" which sounds pretty sinister but also has major "checking into rehab for exhaustion" vibes, which is both glamorous and expensive, so we're withholding judgment. The treatment for white men was probably to smoke more cigarettes.

6 The need to drink water in order to survive is yet another myth we'll be dispelling in our *next* book.

Now if you're thinking, "1869? That was just four years after slavery ended in the United States, and while there was a sense of progress and possibility as free Black people became naturalized citizens, it was also a time of violent racism and backlash to Reconstruction, including Black Codes in the South and the advent of the KKK," then yeah, you're right. If you're thinking, "1869, haha nice," then you have some growing up to do. Seriously. Take a good long look in the mirror; it's enough already. Anyway, like all American History and American Present, the racialized component of neurasthenia or "burnout" is racist, sexist, and underreported—Black Americans, Indigenous Americans, Asian Americans, and other people of color in the country were experiencing mental health issues that shared qualities with the white-centered idea of burnout in addition to the relentless weight of racial marginalization.[7] So while burnout is part of our generational experience with modernity, it plays out differently for everyone. Fortunately, as a satirical publication, we are fully equipped to get to the bottom of this and explain it once and for all.

Normally, reaching something like burnout would be a huge wake-up call that something needs to change in your life, but what if you . . . can't? Not all of us can just quit our day jobs and travel the world or abandon our children with a pack of friendly wolves.[8] Some of us may learn to live with less and cast aside the capitalist notions that things or a particular career will bring us happiness, while others may have never been able to afford those things or ask those questions in the first place. But if there's one thing that we love doing in our culture no matter where we've come from, it's ignoring illness. Remember that time you went to work with a cold that you later found out was COVID, which you later found out you gave to your entire office, and ultimately, the world? Whether you're the COVID bat[9] or just a regular human being, we've been prioritizing work over our weird lower back pain since the dawn of the industrial age as both a means of survival and because we simply can't remember any other way of doing things.

Look, some of us actually love what burnout offers—if it doesn't deliver enviable success, at least you get to work one hundred hours a week, then charge people money to learn how they can work hard without being rich, too. Working yourself to death might be perceived as a bad thing to some people, but it's also a great way to just kind of focus all that negative energy back into work—and isn't that what your parents always wanted for you?

---

7   Hmm, sounds kind of like today!

8   Which is too bad because our cousin's friend was raised by a pack of friendly wolves, and she wrote a totally amazing college admissions essay about it that got her into Stanford.

9   COVID bat had "equity" in a "startup" where "people didn't really take sick days."

They told you to follow your dreams.
Here's why they're wrong.

If you were born somewhere between when wide-leg jeans were cool and when wide-leg jeans were cool again, you were probably told that if you work hard enough, you can achieve your wildest dreams. All you had to do was "work hard" enough to get into college, and regardless of the conditions you were living under, the rest would sort of figure itself out! But only a select few managed to pull that off, and most of *those* people are still paying for it with a side gig, a trust fund, or a side gig plus a smaller trust fund. You know, just like Dad did![10]

A huge part of our culture believes in the myth that any failure is the result of *not working hard enough*. Many great network sitcoms have followed bright, young women trying to have it all, but these stories take place in fictional universes where friends eat breakfast together, like, *before* work (???). We admit, even *Reductress* once believed we could Have It All, but then *Teen Vogue* became a leftist publication and we were, like, totally disillusioned by the myths of capitalism and meritocracy.

It is true that things aren't as easy for our generation: Your parents could pay for college by "mowing lawns in the summer" (what Boomers did before *OnlyFans*), but now you have to take out five and six-figure loans to do the same, if you even have the privilege, support, and luck to be accepted in the first place. And to fill that deficit, we became the *Just Work Harder!* Generation: Our hobbies became work, our social interactions became work, until there was nothing left but sleep (that thing where you close your eyes and have a stress dream about being at work). There was work that was "cool" and less-cool work, and since "cool work" now offered cultural capital, people were willing to be paid less for it, whether they could afford to or not.

Back in those halcyon days of the early 2010s, people were optimistic and things seemed to be going pretty good,[11] but then another generation of young people grew disillusioned with the establishment and realized some truths that predominantly Black and brown scholars and activists had been saying since forever: Success and social mobility are not accessible to all, and the system

---

10 "Dad" is a 25-year-old entrepreneur and son of an oil magnate with a successful CBD toothpaste startup who graduated from Cornell on legacy.

11 Remember your aunt who was all "Sí, se puede" in 2012, and all "I just don't understand why they have to break things" in 2020?

isn't "broken" but rather working exactly as it was designed: to suck for almost everyone who isn't Kylie Jenner.[12] The weight of this knowledge has led many young Americans to feel weird and dye the front strips of their hair pink, and that's not even the worst of it: As technology progressed, life and work began to feel indistinguishable from one another, and so we began to define ourselves through our careers more than anything else.[13] When did we stop just doing something we love for the sake of doing it and working to do the things we love? And is there something we can buy to fix it?

Living in the Moment! This Woman Has No Savings

In this book of incredibly salient and trustworthy advice, we're gonna put a name to all the tiny, almost imperceptible things we've experienced living and working today, the mixed messages we get on how to solve our existential angst, and why so many people make Instagrams for their dogs where the captions are written from the perspective of the dog. And there may be some things in your professional life that you haven't yet put a name to, either, like "benevolent sexism" or "when you know that your coworker is getting paid more than you, but you have to pretend you don't know" or "when you post something on Slack that was like, maybe sort of funny, but not funny enough to share with the whole office, and now you're kind of, like, stressed about it?" Whether it's the politics of your coworking space or the politicians who are

12 And do you really think she's happy? I mean, probably more so than you, but still.
13 And nobody wants to hear about our passion for recreating season 32 of *Survivor* using *Sims* for some reason?

ignoring climate change, there's plenty for you to stress about and plenty of coping mechanisms to feel guilty about, too!

We've established that we're all burnt out, distrustful of the government, and in a state of collective existential crisis (Okay, very '70s! Should we take this to the shag-carpeted conversation pit?), but what can we do? Unfortunately, no one can escape our reality except for that girl from your high school who got really into "spirituality" in a way that feels sort of problematic, but she's always on a mountain or in a natural body of water and doesn't seem to be hurting anyone so you're like, whatever, let her have her hamsa tattoo. But how should *you* be a person in this world? Should you focus on your career and eat Trader Joe's frozen vegan tikka masala for dinner every night?[14] Should you have a bunch of beautiful babies who only wear handsewn frocks and lie on quilts happily snacking on organic fruit, then take pictures of your organic fruit babies and monetize them on Instagram? Should you download the Calm app? It's overwhelming and you're almost definitely getting it wrong, but *Reductress* is here to help, or at least to be just as confused as you are.

---

14 And is Trader Joe's vegan tikka masala just as appropriative as Spirituality Girl's hamsa tattoo? Oh, God.

Chapter 1

Your "Day Job"

"Listing Microsoft Word as a 'skill' on your resume
doesn't mean anything." —Sylvia Plath

If there is one thing this nation was built on, it's exploited labor. Like, really exploited. Like, so exploited that our editor[15] said we weren't allowed to talk about it because it might make white children feel guilty. But whether that labor was being stolen or coerced, workers have always had to advocate for their time and humanity. In the early nineteenth century, unions advocated for better working conditions while regularly working one-hundred-hour weeks. This advocacy involved worker organization, education, and strikes, until employers said, "We hear you and we want to do better. Please, have a two-day weekend and a juicebox." Kidding! Can you imagine? No, they brought in police to beat up the strikers.[16] But these organizers risked their lives and livelihoods over the course of decades to win us one or two of the workers' rights we have today. Isn't America great?

And while we should be grateful to these brave workers who paved the way for many of us to enjoy forty-hour workweeks sitting in little cubicles or an unconscionably large open-concept workspace, these advancements set us up for a whole host of new issues: When do we turn work off? And is this particular job making us crazy or is it just, you know, *gestures broadly* the whole system?

The work/life balance in this country is what experts call "not great" and what the French "don't even have a word for." And while some people prize their all-American monster work ethic,[17] others have to work multiple

---

15 Our editor is an anti-CRT Republican Senator who edits humor books in his free time. We don't always align ideologically, but we have to commend his hustle!

16 There's a reason police unions are so strong: There's nobody else to beat them up.

17 These are the same people who go to Equinox, presumably? We're not allowed in there because we "ate the orange blossoms out of the water cooler" which "aren't even food" and also we're "not members."

minimum-wage jobs and still live below the poverty line, while still others get to work twenty hours a week while pursuing their creative passions until they get kicked off their parents' insurance. Regardless of where you fall on the employment spectrum, the reality is that unless you've been fortunate enough to marry rich in a feminist way or are one of David Beckham's plentiful sons, you probably have to have a job in order to survive. It's a cruel reality, but in this chapter, we'll explore our relationship to our "day job." This might mean deciding the place you spend the majority of your waking hours has nothing to do with who you are, even though every fifteen minutes you kill pretending to check your email is fifteen minutes you're absolutely never getting back in this crazy little thing we call life. Or it could mean hinging your entire identity on climbing the corporate ladder, or the creative ladder, or the regular ladder if you work at a roofing company. Whatever the case, it's going to be bad for your knees.

This Woman Can't Say 'No' to a Job 'Cause She's Afraid She'll Hurt Its Feelings

"I can just do it for, like, two or three years."

Burnout
Through the Ages

10,000 BCE Humans live in a state of idyllic innocence. Based on the artwork, we're fairly sure everyone was having a good time!

8000 BCE The first person to harness modern agriculture becomes sick of the same day-in, day-out bullshit. They also realize they're allergic to gluten :(

3000 BCE Everyone in the cradle of civilization longs to sit down for just one day.

1046 BCE In China, the "Mandate of Heaven" lets the ruling elite of the Zhou dynasty just kind of sit and chill and everyone is like "yeah ok that seems fair, we'll go tend to the rice fields, no problem."

1300 Half of Europe dies because they all just HAD to go to work that day and catch a plague.

1500 The other half of Europe decides every human and natural resource should be extracted for its wealth and that this is a solid long-term strategy.

1789 The ruling class in France is extinguished, which is what happens when a lot of people experience burnout at the same time and decide they "need a big change."

1883 The modern notion of time is invented so that trains can run "on time," giving people something to be anxious about other than cholera.

1917 The first time the U.S. government pretends there isn't a pandemic going on, proving denial is a flawless coping mechanism.

1957 Someone invents the washing machine, giving rich women more free time to develop an addiction to benzos.

1974 Two Boomers independently think they "discover" burnout, as the ideals of the '60s begin to feel unattainable in the face of society's problems.

1980 Boomers decide that the real problem was the "having ideals" part.

1994 *Friends* invents being a comfort show that simultaneously gives you anxiety because the characters' apartments are huge even though they mostly work in food service.

2009 A recession lets 10 percent of the population take a nice, long, unpaid break for once.

2012 Smartphones and clinical depression finally become mainstream.

2016 A white supremacist rapist becomes president and people take to the streets to revolt! But then they get off the streets because they have to go to work.

2020 The last fucking straw. People decide they're not gonna take this toxic productivity culture and dysfunctional country anymore.

2022 We mean it this time!!

2023 . . .

HOW TO DEAL WITH YOUR SEXIST DIGESTIVE SYSTEM TALKING OVER YOU DURING MEETINGS

Getting your voice heard as a woman in the workplace can be difficult, especially when you have to share space with toxic people and organs that have no qualms with unabashedly talking over you in meetings. These types of coworkers can make work a drag and make you feel unheard, but, luckily, there are approaches you can take to rise above this sort of harmful behavior. Here are some tips to deal with that asshole sexist digestive system that won't stop talking over you during meetings.

Proactively silence it.

If you don't want your large intestine moaning and groaning like the misogynist it is while you try to contribute a stellar point during a team meeting, you need to plan ahead. Stick to the BRAT diet (bananas, rice, applesauce, and toast) to keep things mum. This regimen is generally reserved for those trying to stop having diarrhea, but even if you're regular, this should probably just ensure that nothing is stirring and bubbling around in your colon or whatever it is that makes those embarrassing, undermining sounds that take away your sense of agency in the workplace. If you're worried about the long-term effects of such a nutritionally limited diet, then maybe you're not cut out to fight tooth-and-nail in a male dominated field! Oh, your field isn't male-dominated? You work in fashion? All the same.

Call out unacceptable behavior.

It's a tough burden to bear, but change doesn't just happen without brave people speaking up. When you're delivering an eloquent point in a team meeting and your stomach begins to release a wild growl, look down and sternly say, "Hey! I am talking right now and you need to wait your turn." Repeatedly speaking to your stomach could lead people to believe that you're crazy (bad for your career) or pregnant (worse!), but your coworkers need to know that you're not the type to let others walk all over you. Also, no one is going to respect you if it seems like you're trying to make a point while holding in a fart.

Scream.

Michelle Obama once said, "When they go low, we go high," which we take to mean, when your stomach makes a weird, low sound, scream in a much higher pitch. Your screams are sure to positively redirect attention and drown out the embarrassing sound of your digestive system simply doing its job after a meal with unexpected dairy. Of course, screaming bloody murder during a team meeting might lead your coworkers to believe they are in immediate danger and crisis. The good news is, if everyone does an emergency evacuation of the office because they assume you saw a shooter or are possessed by the Dark Lord, they'll never think, "Wow, what a doormat. We can definitely steal her ideas and not take her seriously." Better to be feared than interrupted by sexist gas!

Being a woman in the workplace still comes with plenty of unique challenges, but these creative solutions allow you to show your team who's boss. Hopefully one day we'll be able to upload our consciousnesses to the cloud and not have our productivity impeded by having to exist in a body, but until then, keep screaming!

TIP:
Set Boundaries by Only Checking Your Email at Every Other Stoplight

---

Congratulations! You Are Reading a Book

Look at you! You're reading a book! You put all distractions aside to finally sit down and focus on a singular activity that will finally let your brain do the thing it was meant to do: think, process, and reflect on pages of words! This reading thing isn't easy, and you should be proud of the fact that you didn't pick up your phone when you got that text message just now. You didn't pick it up, right? Of course not; you're reading! Well, have fun!

HOW I ENHANCED MY RESUME BY USING STRONG ACTION WORDS LIKE "FUCK"

By McKayley Gourley

If you're in the job market—or looking to be soon—it's essential to make the most out of your resume. Hiring managers are constantly bombarded with applications, so in order to stand out and catch their eye, you need to make every word on your resume count.

One of the first things I did to optimize my resume was to get rid of my lackluster descriptors—words like "helped" and "assisted"—and instead opt for stronger, more compelling action words like "cultivated," "achieved," or "coordinated."

While the results from this transition were great (I started to receive rejections of my job applications, whereas before, it was radio silence), they weren't as dramatic as I had hoped.

So I took it a step further: This time, when I took a red pen to my resume, I not only weeded out the weak, passive descriptors, but I re-evaluated my so-called "strong" descriptors as well. I immediately realized they knew they weren't as compelling as they could be. The only viable next step was to use what my mom would call "very strong language."

I wanted to convey agency in my work, as well as the extent of my contributions. So, this time, I replaced my humble helping words with descriptors that no longer undercut my work or diminished my accomplishments. I substituted my ill-placed humility with something guaranteed to set me apart from the other candidates—an abrasive, borderline confrontational overconfidence cultivated by a resume littered with powerful action words such as "fuck."

Instead of "cultivated"—I opted for "fucking cultivated."

Instead of "achieved"—"fucking achieved."

Instead of "coordinated"—"did fucking everything for this hellhole of a company."

These small changes instantly took my resume from somewhat "weak" and "unremarkable" to undeniably "unhinged." And hiring managers liked that. Well, maybe not liked, but certainly respected. Or, if not respected, at the very least, feared. Which is precisely what I wanted, and what today's competitive, cutthroat job market demands. Other times, people just assumed that anyone with such a flagrant disregard for institutions was surely an antisocial Silicon Valley genius or child of A-list celebs: both highly in demand. Of course, I'm neither, but no one's catching on to that when I'm employing brilliant resume tricks like continually saying "fuck" or writing "fuck" in slightly differing font sizes to assault their senses and send them into a vulnerable state of confusion and terror.

By injecting my resume with strong action words like, for example: "fuck," "fucking" and "fucked,"—as well as letting my blatant disdain for my employers past and present bleed into my words—I enhanced the tone of my resume, showing hiring managers that I was not some passive, listless applicant, but instead a deranged maniac who harbors a palpable disdain for everyone they've ever worked for and all the work they've ever done. In short—it was an instant improvement.

After seamlessly adopting this approach into every aspect of my resume, I found myself outlining pointers for others who might be looking to employ this strategy and take back the power in the hiring process:

If you managed a team:

Instead of listing off your managerial duties with tired phrases like "managed people" or "led a team"—try inserting some zest into your resume with devastating descriptors like:

1. Did Fucking Everything
2. Utilized a Cunty Attitude to Inspire Action
3. Employed a Stringent "No Dicking Around" Policy

If you took the lead on a project:

If you were the lead on a company initiative, replace "led" with stronger verbs like "controlled," "managed," or "chaired"—and then slap a well-placed expletive in front of them to show hiring managers, quite simply, that you're not fucking around, like so:

1. Fucking Controlled
2. Fucking Managed
3. Fucking Made That Shit My Absolute Bitch

If you saved the company time and money:

Hiring managers are obsessed with candidates who have saved their companies time and money, and even more obsessed with those who did it with an attitude of violence.

1. Consolidated the Hell Out of Costs
2. Conserved a Fuck-Ton of Resources
3. Decreased Expenses for Those Slimy, Bourgeois Fucks I Toil Beneath

By utilizing the above examples, you'll show hiring managers that you know your worth, and maybe even vastly overestimate it.

At the end of the day, it's just important to remember that it's okay to brag a bit on your resume (while simultaneously slandering your past bosses and workplaces as you do so). Hiring managers love bold authenticity, and nothing is more authentic than speaking about your work in the crude, bitter way you complain to your friends.

It is my hope that other job seekers will follow my lead and let their authentic selves shine through in their resumes—their verbally belligerent selves, complete with spiteful hearts and filthy mouths. Good fucking luck!

> **TIP:**
> **Make Being Busy More Fun by Spelling It "Bizzy." Haha! Did that work?**

NICE! THIS WOMAN JOINED A NONPROFIT TO FUNDRAISE FOR HER OWN SALARY

By Mai Tran

In a remarkable show of commitment to vulnerable and underserved populations, Sarah Chen left her well-paying corporate law job to join a nonprofit, where she now works long hours reaching out to wealthy donors in order to fundraise for her own salary.

"I feel so much freer," Chen said. "Doing pro-bono work was the highlight of my former job, and now I'm excited to spend as much as 20 percent of my time at work advocating for and working with people who look like me."

After a one-month onboarding process that involved interfacing with several white women, signing multiple liability waivers, and giving Chen access to the organization's shared accounts because it couldn't afford to make individual ones, Chen started her new job as a Field Associate, where she spends 65 percent of her time applying for grants simply so she can continue working.

"Next week, I'm organizing a panel on warehouse workers' union and labor rights," said Chen. "This is a priority issue for me because so many corporations are exploiting workers and they don't even know it's happening."

"I'm so glad Sarah is taking the lead on making events more inclusive and pushing the organization in a more progressive direction," said Executive Director Kristi Kline. "We are committed to diversity, equity, and inclusion, which Sarah does a great job at!"

Although slow and unresponsive departments might discourage some people from dedicating the majority of their lives to a company, Chen isn't like the other workers.

"I just feel like I can make a big impact here," she said. "This work is so necessary. If I don't do it, who will? Literally, who will fundraise for my salary?"

If Chen's altruism is ever discouraged by the long hours and low pay, she is quickly relieved by free Chobani yogurt, tote bags, pens, and beer coozies that randomly appear on her desk from the Board of Directors, which definitely makes up for the lack of health insurance.

In between her daytime emails and her nighttime emails, Chen is working on an annual grant that will allow her to continue working at the organization for another year.

When prompted to state what she would do with the money, Chen was well prepared to answer.

"I am dedicated to my organization's mission statement, to create a just and equitable society and be a voice for the voicele—"

"Sarah? If you're not busy, could you help translate something for me?"

After a short interlude to act as a translator for Kline, Chen returned to her grant application.

"I used to represent people who destroyed the rainforest, but now I'm subverting the narrative by using their private profits to fund my own salary. Other people are cogs in the machine, but I'm dismantling the machine because if I don't get funding, I will not have a job in three months."

Consider us inspired!

Woman Who Joined Nonprofit Job to Make the World a Better Place Spends Most of Job Sucking Up to Donors Who Are Making the World a Much Worse Place

HOW TO MAKE YOUR HOME WORKPLACE SAFER

By Seth Rubin

Setting up and maintaining a home workplace can be an exciting prospect for any remote worker. But an oft-overlooked aspect of any home office is that of workplace safety, which is just as important in the corner of a bedroom as it is on a factory floor. Read on to learn about how you can ensure that your work-from-home setup is as safe as it is productive!

Hire an OSHA supervisor.

OSHA, or the Occupational Safety and Health Administration, is a government organization designed to help keep workplaces safe. Haven't had another human being in your home in months? No problem! Consider knitting a neon green vest and a little OSHA badge for your beloved pet and train them to help keep you safe. Teaching a rescue dog to blow a whistle every time you misuse a stapler may take time, but the results will speak for themselves.

> Did you know? *Many pet birds know how to dial 911 now.*
> *That means an entire flock of pet birds can dial 911 many times!*

Protect yourself from hazardous chemicals.

You may not be mixing up hazardous chemicals at home, but the piping-hot coffee you're chugging at your desk can still cause burns, jitteriness, and even acid reflux, which does *not* make for a safe workplace. Sure, sometimes you just need a little java to start writing your signature erotic Timothée Chalamet/Mewtwo fanfiction on your lunch break, but whenever your workload is less demanding, consider switching to warm green tea!

> **Did you know?** *Mewtwo is known to have the most savage heart of any Pokémon, but it can be calmed by Timothée's soulful gaze.*

Know your emergency exits.

If there's an emergency, do you know how to safely leave your bedroom? I mean, of course, the door, you know that, but—oh, you know that the window works, too? Okay. No, it's fine. I'm just trying to help people here, but you already know things. Let's just move on.

> **Did you know?** *Many home workplace safety enthusiasts scored really high on their SATs, even if their grades weren't good enough for Doctors Without Borders, and they still deserve your respect.*

Invest in PPE.

Personal protective equipment, or PPE, is a workplace staple. Consider investing in ergonomic keyboards and chairs to help keep your body limber and cramp-free.

> **Did you know?** *"Limber and cramp-free" can also describe Timothée Chalamet and Mewtwo in your fanfiction! Consider having your two heroes meet in a tumbling gym or physical therapy clinic instead of an oil refinery.*

Use caution when operating machinery.

To be specific: Do not bring a toaster in the bath with you because you think it would be fun to make bath toast.

> **Did you know?** *Over 75 remote employees die every year after succumbing to the siren song of that sweet, sweet bath toast.*

Protect yourself from falls.

If you're going to masturbate to the Timothée Chalamet/Mewtwo fanfiction you're writing instead of doing the data entry job you're being paid to do, at least do it lying down. Hundreds of remote workers every year injure themselves in their home offices by falling down during the throes of passion while precariously balancing on a stack of loose paperwork.

> **Did you know?** *Unlike remote employees, Timothée and Mewtwo can spend hours exploring each other's bodies without needing to stop for food and water.*

Watch your posture.

It's not good, is it? Don't lie to us. You work from home! How do you have the crumpled body of a sea-battered longshoreman? Sit up straight!

> **Did you know?** *Many home workplace safety enthusiasts don't mean to yell. And yet, just like so many other workers, we find ourselves turning into our parents as we approach middle age . . .*

Take breaks.

Whether you're operating a forklift or using your laptop to describe the gentle cascade of Timothée Chalamet's curls on Mewtwo's grayish-purple skin, a well-rested worker has a better chance of facing obstacles and setbacks without getting injured. Give yourself time during the day to rest, ponder, and reflect before returning to work.

> **Did you know?** *When Timothée Chalamet locked eyes with Mewtwo across the crowded museum gift shop, the Oscar-nominated actor wasn't looking for anything serious. But as he watched the three-fingered, 6'7" alien cat inspect a Frida Kahlo novelty mug, he could feel a familiar sensation growing in the pit of his stomach: a thirst that only Mewtwo could quench.*

Report workplace safety violations.

If your pet birds aren't dialing 911 every time you fall down while masturbating, or if your workplace safety cat hasn't yet learned how to differentiate the gentle sizzling of bath toast from the quiet whirr of an ergonomic chair, you may need to reach out to a workplace safety organization to report such violations. Be sure to be specific and detailed to provide data that can help keep millions of other remote workers safe!

> **Did you know?** Timothée Chalamet ran his elegant fingers down Mewtwo's phallic tail. "Mewtwo," said Mewtwo, angling its hips upward. The Psychic-type Legendary Pokémon let out a low moan as the Dune star brushed his delicate ringlets out of his piercing hazel eyes. "Mewtwo," said Timothée, "We can explore each other's bodies now because our home workplace is safe." "Mewtwo," said Mewtwo.

So there you have it: nine simple, easy ways to ensure that your at-home workspace is just as safe as any brick-and-mortar establishment. Follow these steps and you'll end up with a safe, erotically charged home office that will be the envy of your virtual coworkers!

Productivity Advice from Boomer Dad

"If you really want a job, start knocking on the doors of every company, march right in there, and hand them your resume. Don't forget to give a firm handshake and look them in the eye. Then, slide under the door as if you are a liquid. They'll be impressed, and you'll be buying a five-bedroom house, all-cash, in two months."

DIVERSITY WIN! THIS COMPANY HIRED ONE BIRACIAL PERSON AND CALLED HER "DIVERSITY"

Nobody takes diversity more seriously than Silicon Valley, and AI startup Winston Logistics is no exception: This company took their diversity initiatives to the next level and hired one biracial person for their fifty-person team—and now they're all done with the diversity thing!

Thirty-year-old software engineer Shaina Campbell is half-Black, half-Jewish, and has absolutely no idea that she is the entirety of her company's diversity initiative.

"I know this industry has a huge race problem and a gender problem, too," says Shaina. "I just didn't know I'd have to solve all of those things with my presence. Or that when their HR department says the company is 'diverse' that they're literally talking about me."

All it takes is one person, we guess!

"It took a long time for us to recruit the right pool of talent for Winston," says HR director Katie Moss. "And I'm over the moon that we could finally bring some diversity to our growing team in the form of Diversity—I mean, Shaina. Her name is Shaina. God, I really need to stop doing that."

In addition to leading the development of the company's groundbreaking AI software, Shaina has also enjoyed being the "sounding board" on issues from racial bias in technology to the company's official stance on Israel.

"I was not hired to do this," says Shaina. "I'm making $250,000 a year, and it is still not enough."

As Winston grows, the team hopes they can become even more "diverse."

"Diversity is important to our company," added Katie. "Which is why we just promoted Shaina to be our Head of Diversity in charge of hiring, growth, development, and corporate diversity initiatives, making us more diverse than ever."

"Wow," Shaina said about the promotion. "As a software engineer, I have no idea what that job even is."

When asked what's next in their company initiatives, Katie stalled, then brought Shaina into a last-minute meeting to ask what "inclusion" means.

Way to break that glass ceiling, Shaina!

HOW WORKING A BRUNCH SHIFT ENDED MY RELATIONSHIP WITH GOD

Though the metropolitan centers of our nation are increasingly secular, I myself have always managed to maintain a close relationship to grace and divinity through faith. My faith in the Lord God helped me through myriad trials, such as battling a rare childhood autoimmune disease in middle school and finding street parking in the city, but that all changed when I agreed to cover my coworker's weekend brunch shift: A decision that would come to end my relationship with our alleged Lord and Savior.

As a server, I generally worked evenings, providing patrons with dinner: a justified and decent meal. In the cool dark of night, I would take my short breaks, smoking a cigarette in the alley with the line cook and communing with Him in moments of peace and reflection. But when my coworker asked me to take over his brunch shift so he could go to a live taping of *The View* for "career reasons," I figured I would be a good Samaritan and do just that.

Now I know that God is dead and we have killed Him.

Brunch, like French Bulldogs and nuclear war, is a human creation made to torment the Lord. It's a sprawling expanse of chaos from the start of normal breakfast time till the end of normal lunchtime, during which people are compelled to spend $26 on French toast and drink champagne in the morning. Like most things that make God cry, I'm pretty sure it was invented by Australians.

Job, a righteous man in the Old Testament, found his inner strength and ultimate faith in the Lord after enduring a series of devastating trials. However, Job never had to serve table 4, an eight-top where additional people kept joining over the course of their three-hour meal, despite the fact that we only seat complete parties. One such straggler was a woman with a son who she insisted needed a booster seat even though he was, like, nine. Then she asked if he could have some crayons and paper, neither of which we have, so I gave him a pen and some old receipts, upon which he proceeded to draw some incredibly anti-Irish Liberation cartoons. Eventually, the child appeared drunk on bottomless mimosas. The whole thing was just a nightmare.

I held on to my faith for dear life, praying for grace, calm, and, above all, an end to the madness. And I almost made it, too, but then a guy with a $120 check left what he didn't finish of his *croque madame* as a "tip," at which point I renounced religion and became a social Darwinist.

As for what's next, I may go off the grid or perhaps run the Iditarod (no dogs, just me and my newfound atheistic rage over the futility of existence). At the very least, I'll stick to dinner shifts, because all the evils of humanity on display are slightly less disturbing when it's not a drunken weekend afternoon.

AW! THIS STARTUP HAS JUST BEEN SITTING "WHEREVER" AND NOW THEY ALL HAVE BACK PROBLEMS

In an inspiring story of innovation and shifting office culture, employees of the Seattle-based mobile startup, Pawz, have just been sitting kind of "wherever" in a sprawling open office for over eight years—and amazingly, now they each have a host of complex back problems.

"This whole thing was just a dream I had in undergrad at Berkeley," says thirty-year-old Pawz creator and CEO Riley Haverford, shifting around in a plastic chair. "Sorry, what was I saying? Pawz . . . dream I had at Berkeley. Yeah, no it's cool to have a whole operation built around this now. God, I'm in so much pain."

What began as one computer science student's vision now includes an ambitious and diverse team of coders, graphic designers, and social media marketers, who collectively decided against a traditional office layout and now all have strained lower discs in their young lumbar spines.

"Yeah, we've got some bean bags, some stools in the kitchen area, and that swing in the corner that we've all taken some sick 'grams in, but is pretty easy to fall off of," says Haverford, walking through the open office space. "And then we have a ping pong table that some people try to use as a standing desk, but it's not that tall so they kind of just get on their knees or hunch over it."

"We probably should have gotten more office chairs," Haverford adds. "But did you know that they are, like, hundreds and hundreds of dollars? Plus, we already bought the swing and the ping pong table."

"Anyway, depending on Q2 numbers, I'm gonna try to get a massage day for everyone," says Haverford. "Sure, none of the spine doctors or physical therapists in this state take our insurance, but it's something!"

And a radical lack of lumbar support isn't the only way Pawz is disrupting the norms of American work culture.

"Part of what drew me to this position was the fluidity of the hours," says Pawz chief graphic designer Ophelia Yi. "We don't do the whole 9-to-5 thing here. I come in around 10, and if I wanted to take a long lunch or go to the gym in the middle of the day, I totally could, not that I've ever done that. Then I leave around 8, or 9 p.m., or whenever I can without being the first to call it a day.

"Plus through Pawz I get an Uber discount," Yi adds. "Which is great because I used to bike to work but now I can't because I don't have full range of motion in my neck."

We love to see young people making work work for them!

"It's just chill vibes here," says Haverford, passing along a tub of Icy Hot to another programmer. "And we're all brought together by a shared belief in the work we're doing."

"What is Pawz? Well it's more of an ethos," Haverford says. "But if I had to distill it into words, I guess those words would be: a meditation app for dogs."

The future is now!

Productivity Advice from Boomer Dad

"Every household needs a toolbox. Put it somewhere safe, because if your kid opens it, you'll switch bodies. Then you'll have to go to your kid's college classes, which will be satisfying, because you'll prove that their life is actually easy, but who has the time?"

HOW TO WRITE THE PERFECT EMAIL THAT CONVEYS YOUR BRAIN IS NO LONGER IN YOUR BODY

By Freddie Shanel

Crafting the perfect email can make a sane person want to puke, even in normal circumstances, and it can be even harder to do when you've worked so many hours that your brain officially left your body about two hours to two years ago, give or take. How are you supposed to summarize your thoughts into a colloquial yet professional package when your thoughts themselves have, for all intents and purposes, become detached from the rest of you? Here's a step-by-step guide for writing the perfect email that at once gets your point across *and* conveys that your brain is no longer in your body!

Start strong with, "Apologies for the delay—I fear my brain is no longer in my body."

The classics are classics for a reason, and this email salutation is the *Catcher in the Rye* of conveying that your brain is no longer in your body. It's got everything: an apology, a direct statement, and an excuse that absolutely no one can deny. Why skirt around the issue that you've been "kind of off" for two straight years when you can come right out and say it up top? The receiver of this email will likely be floored by your honesty and, frankly, a little bit turned on.

Follow that up with a lighthearted joke!

The key to living through unprecedented circumstances is learning how to diffuse tension. If your opening statement says, "Whoa, this person is going through it," the following joke should say, "but in a kind of funny way! Like in a chill way that is relatable and entertaining to me." Genuine concern? That's scary. I'm scared. Genuine concern followed by joke? Now, that's content, baby!

Throw a good "Hahahahahahahahahaha" somewhere in the middle.

Nothing like a Joker-style email laugh to communicate that you're afraid for yourself and your future. This phrase says, "Please don't fault me for taking six weeks to respond to an email that would reasonably take anyone else twenty-four hours. I have been unwell, mentally." This short addition is a testament to how so few words can say so much, like, "Please help? My brain is just on my bedside table next to my body."

Take a quick break from what you're saying with this digression: "Hark! What light from yonder window breaks!"

In email world, we call this "showing, not telling." Sure, any old email could *say* "my brain isn't in my body anymore," but how many emails can *show* it? It'll have your reader (yeah, we believe emails are literature), saying, "What?? Huh?? Weren't we talking about something else?" And that's right where you want them. This email screams, "member of the literati," but more importantly, it just screams.

Right when it seems you're getting into the meat of your email, instead say, "Let's cut the shit, Greg. I don't want to be here; you don't want to be here. Let's make a baby."

This part is pretty self-explanatory, but for the sake of clarity, let's dive in: This kind of direct address will really take your reader by surprise if their name is Greg, and even more so if not. The phrase "Let's cut the shit," suggests you mean business, perhaps even in a cold way, but the phrase, "Let's make a baby," will bring them right back in. Email writing is a game of cat and mouse, an ebb and flow like waves lapping the shore. It can be scary to be vulnerable like this, to cut through all the niceties that distract us from the dire state of our world, but it'll all be worth it when your email recipient comprehends that your brain is no longer in your body, but perhaps in a jar nearby, or simply spilled all over the kitchen floor.

Finish strong with, "Ungggggg."

This one takes some creative liberties, but boy does it get the job done. Sure, you could wax poetic about *why* your brain is missing from your body and *how* that makes you feel and *where* you think your brain might be, but who has time for that? A quick "Ungggggg" says what normal words never could: "Are we really doing this now? We're spending our one God-given life writing emails? Isn't your daughter's ballet recital happening right now? It isn't? Well, why not?"

Sign it, "Cheers, {your name}"

It's the kind of flippant and unhinged sign-off that'll make it super clear you're mentally gone.

There you have it! You're ready to write the perfect email for any occasion, as long as the occasion is the end of days, and the message is that you just can't do this anymore. Go forth and write, friend! We hope one day you recognize yourself in the mirror again, but as always, no worries if not. It should be noted that the person you're sending this email to will likely respond, "K." But isn't that what life's all about?

How to Reject Productivity Culture Without Falling Behind Your Peers and Colleagues

- Redefine success by thinking about how humiliating it is to try.

- Stop spending time comparing yourself to others and use that time to publicly belittle their accomplishments and endeavors.

- Recognize how hustling may be ruining your brain but never your reputation.

- Make rejecting productivity culture your brand, then gain a fuckload of followers from posting about it.

- Tell yourself four to five hours of sleep is actually the right amount for you.

WHY THE U.S. NEEDS BETTER PUBLIC TRANSIT FOR US TO JUMP IN FRONT OF

If there's one issue that makes commuting unbearable, unpredictable, and unaffordable for the average American, it's that our national infrastructure is crumbling—especially our underfunded public transit systems. For those of us who still travel to work, trains are slow, dirty, and rarely reach areas where people are most in need of reliable transit to get to the job they hate on time.

The U.S. lags far behind other developed nations full of similarly miserable people, but with far more beautiful high-speed trains you could jump directly in front of if you really felt like it.

It's time we do better, America.

Our country has disinvested in public transit for decades, and now, many working adults wonder if they'll be fired from their job due to one late train or an unexpected traffic jam on dilapidated roads. Reliable public transit would give us our time back, so we can be like every other developed nation that gets to stand on a sparkling train platform with clearly marked signage where we can contemplate whether any of this is really worth it.

Why do we have to be miserable and late while the rest of the developed world is miserable and on time?

Reliable public transit isn't just safer, it helps make people more productive: Countries like Japan have such high-quality public transit that trains leave on-the-minute—unless, of course, someone jumps in front of one and then there's a huge delay. But that is rare! Most people just kind of think about it, but the trains come so fast that they forget.

Trains in Europe and Asia are also immaculate on the inside and out; something that New Yorkers or San Franciscans could only ever dream of jumping in front of.

Now, I know what you might be thinking: We don't even have reliable healthcare in America! With everything going on in the world, why should we even bother building a better train system for us to contemplate "what if" as it careens into the station? It's because our public transit is a reflection of us as a country. Is America just going to continue being "every man for himself"? Or can we find the collective courage to build something better so we can briefly indulge the fantasy of ending it all on a slightly more European level?

I'm not saying that we should, but it's nice to know that we could if we wanted to.

After all, we may all be exhausted, burnt out, and unable to cope with daily life wherever we are in the developed world, but with better public infrastructure, we too can join the rest of the great nations with better, safer, and faster modes of self-destruction than ever before. Here's to the future!

Productivity Advice from Boomer Dad

"Get a good filing cabinet to keep all your receipts. You never know when the government is gonna come and take your guns and you're gonna need to show all the receipts for your guns."

HOW TO FOCUS ON REMOTE WORK WHEN THE WOMAN IN YOUR WALLPAPER KEEPS BEGGING YOU TO FREE HER

By Heven Haile

At a time when it feels like we're constantly living through the climax of a dumpster fire, the ability to work remotely has been a huge silver lining for many of us. The elimination of exhausting daily commutes and expensive work meals left many better resourced than ever before. However, it also left us with more opportunities to become distracted by the strange woman who haunts the walls of our homes. If you're desperately looking for a way to focus on your work assignments despite the sound of a trapped soul clawing at you from within your walls, you're in luck! Here are some tips and tricks to stay on task and boost your productivity even as the tortured woman in your wallpaper demands that you free her from her eternal prison.

Position your desk facing a window.

With your gaze fixed upon the outside world, you can focus on your plans for career growth and ignore the constant scratching underneath the wallpaper behind you. You can also use this as an opportunity to take advantage of the natural lighting over Zoom. The warm glow from the sun will distract your coworkers from the shadowy figure in the background whispering, "Help meeee" throughout the workday.

Wear headphones.

Put on your chunkiest noise-canceling headphone to drown out the nightly wails and daily groans of your tortured guest. To get a full night's rest, try some calming ocean sounds, or perhaps Harry Styles reading you a bedtime story on the Calm app. During the day, try some lo-fi beats or classical music. Maybe some slow + reverb Frank Ocean songs will make the pleading woman in your wallpaper chill out, too. Remember—the music from her time wasn't very good.

Invest in a room divider!

Give her some privacy, Jesus. Chances are she's been there longer than you. Imagine how she feels watching you stare at her.

Look into support groups for people with the same affliction.

Who knows, your neighbor might be living with their own wallpaper woman and you're both just too afraid to say her name out loud (this is the one thing that would break her curse and free her from your antique wallpaper). If you find out that one lives across the street, you can set up little tin can phone lines for them to use! Give them a curfew, though, or you'll hear their tinny, muffled groans all night long!

Ask her to take your spot in Zoom meetings.

It's not like she has anything else to do! She's probably super bored and could use a bit of social stimulation! Just make sure you turn off your camera.

Create a joint YouTube channel.

If you don't capitalize on this moment, someone else will! Perhaps she has some good true crime tales to share about her own gruesome murder or a soothing yet subtly haunting voice that's perfect for ASMR. There's a market for everything! You won't even need to worry about remote work anymore once you find a way to monetize your wall ghost.

Develop a whirlwind romance!

Think of this like you're in a Victorian romance novel. You could etch love notes to each other on your walls and you don't have to worry about being ghosted because she literally can't leave. Plus, if things end poorly, you can simply move! Make sure not to tell them about the jilted, heartbroken woman living in your wallpaper.

Try to free her by clawing at your wallpaper until your fingers turn into bloody stumps.

Don't give up! She's really in there! After working alone in your room for over three years, you're definitely not currently experiencing a mental break caused by extended periods of isolation and stress. Wait? Oh no! She's in deeper than you thought. Try a hammer? Who would've thought your soulmate would turn out to be a person living in your walls? Talk about forbidden love. There is a way you can join her . . .

Pass away from the heartbreak of being separated from your one true love and join her in the wallpaper.

The best thing about it is that you won't have to answer another Slack message ever again.

If nothing else works: Suggest that she pay rent.

Let's face it: You've probably lost your job by now, and she's still not going anywhere. You might as well treat her like a roommate. And like any roommate, she must contribute her fair share. This might actually cause her to realize that late-stage capitalism is far more terrifying than whatever she's going through and motivate her to finally cross over into the spirit realm. Win-win!

Promotion Comes with Salary Increase That Just Covers Therapy Needed to Survive Promotion

Productivity Advice from Boomer Dad

"They say not to eat before a colonoscopy, but they won't hassle you over a turkey sandwich."

HOW TO EXPLAIN TO YOUR BOSS THAT YOU DON'T HAVE THOSE REPORTS 'CAUSE WE'RE ALL GOING TO DIE SOMEDAY

Is it Friday afternoon and your boss is wondering about that long-term project you've been painstakingly avoiding for three weeks? First of all: Good job! More importantly, you're probably wondering how to explain to her that you don't have them right now because we're ultimately going to die someday, and we should all go outside and touch the sweet spring grass while we still can. But how do you put that in a way that she'll understand so that you don't have to write those reports? Here's how to give a casual reminder that you don't have them because life is so beautiful and brief:

Remind her of the fragility of existence.

This one is great whether you've got something due or not—remind your boss via Slack or email that human existence is incredibly fragile and could be wiped out in an instant. If you feel weird about writing it out, find a funny meme and just send it with zero explanation! She'll laugh, but then she'll *think*. Hopefully she shuts her laptop for good and tells you she appreciates you for the loving reminder. If you're lucky, she'll give you a warm hug and tell you to go appreciate the fragile beauty of a flower. She certainly won't be asking about those reports!

Tell her that she surely won't be thinking about those reports on her deathbed.

This one might come off a little harsh, but if she really thinks about it, she'll ultimately agree that you are right: She will *definitely* not be thinking about the mounting tasks at work you haven't done in the past three months when her life flashes before her on her deathbed! Just make sure to say it in a way that doesn't sound like a threat. This is also a great time to put in a vacation request!

Remind her of the things that really matter.

Sure, she's your boss and she's supposed to give you work to do—we all get it! But everyone needs a reminder that meaningful human connection is worth more than any silly report that determines the entirety of next year's hiring plan. Look her deeply in the eye, give her a smile, and say, "Hey, this connection we have right here? This is all we got." When she ultimately agrees (who wouldn't?), you can get back to watching videos of adorable kittens with birth defects in the bathroom. You've earned it!

Be specific and direct.

When she asks you outright if you have the reports ready because they are due today, don't be afraid to tell her the brutally honest truth: "Look, Kayleigh, I know you probably don't think about this a lot, but each and every one of us is going to die. And you know what? That shouldn't make us sad; it should *inspire us to truly live*." Once she has a moment to let that sink in, she should rip off her heels, throw her laptop out the window, and head for the exit as she frantically tells strangers, "I love you." That's the perfect chance to take a nap!

You may not totally get through to her at first, but with some consistency, you should wear her down to the point where she'll just kind of let you vibe at your desk for a few months while still getting paid. After all, isn't that what life is all about?

Productivity Advice from Boomer Dad

"Don't sleep in on the weekends; there's always something to be done. Get up and do some yard work. Mow your lawn. Make friends with the squirrels. Give the squirrels a bath. Hug them and tell them you're proud of them, unlike your lazy, piece-of-shit children. What do you mean you don't have a 'yard'?"

MEET THE WOMAN WORKING A JOB SHE HATES TO IMPRESS PEOPLE SHE DOESN'T RESPECT

We love to spotlight women who embody a blend of strong work ethic and core values, and there's no better candidate than Molly Tanaka-Cohen: a woman working a job she absolutely fucking hates to impress people she doesn't respect at all.

While Molly is now a successful casting agent in Los Angeles, striking jealousy and admiration into the hearts of people who will never love her, she didn't always have such a perfect life.

"When I first graduated, I was sort of floating, unsure what I wanted to do with myself," Molly says. "When I first got a job at a reputable casting agency, I knew I didn't love it and thought it would be temporary. I mean, the hours were insane and I felt no personal calling toward the work."

But that all changed when Molly caught wind of a casual acquaintance talking shit about her.

"This friend of mine said that she ran into this girl who lived on our floor freshman year of college," Molly says. "And she was like, 'I'm really surprised that Molly is among the first of us to have a real career; she never seemed that serious about school or anything.' And that's when I knew: This bitch is jealous, and I will do anything to keep her that way."

"When I realized that from the outside, my life seemed impressive to a person I don't really know, like, or respect, it was all the motivation I needed to keep going," Molly adds. "So when I got a nominal promotion that meant more work for the same amount of money, I was thrilled."

While Molly has considered making changes to increase her enjoyment of life, there is ultimately little external motivation from her haters to do so.

"I've always wanted to work with children, and I've thought about going back to school to get a degree in education and leaving LA for good," she says. "But I don't want people who I would have never been in contact with if it weren't for social media to think that I couldn't hack it out here, so I'll probably just keep grinding until I get verified on Twitter or when the climate crisis renders this region uninhabitable. Whichever comes first!"

We stan a worker bee with immaculate priorities. Keep appearing to thrive while internally crumbling, Molly! It's totally worth it!

Productivity Advice from Boomer Dad

"Invest in a car that's reliable and not too show-offy. You don't want to break down in the middle of the night coming home late from work, where a mysterious man will come help look at your engine, but when you turn around he's gone and you realize he was a ghost. That won't happen if you get a Camry."

MY SERVICE JOB DOESN'T HAVE INSURANCE, BUT I DO HAVE A CAREER WAITER COWORKER WHO I THINK MIGHT BE PSYCHIC

As a creative working part-time in the service industry, it likely comes as no surprise that my job doesn't offer insurance. Like so many young artists, the flexibility and vivacity of a restaurant job gives me the space to pursue my true passion, but it doesn't offer the cushy comforts of your standard 9-to-5. But whether front or back of house, there's a special breed of camaraderie that comes with this line of work. So no, I don't have health insurance, but I do have a career waiter coworker who I'm pretty sure is psychic, so do I *really* need it?

I've asked him directly, and he agrees that I don't.

My coworker Byron is a statuesque, mid-forties, neatly mustachioed gay man who is a genius. Nobody knows how long he has been a waiter at the French bistro where I work as a host, but presumably the answer is forever. Perhaps he was once an actor, perhaps he was once a dancer, perhaps he has always been a highly competent waiter who makes customers feel like the purpose of their dining experience is to pass a test he is administering. And if that weren't enough, I have gathered enough evidence that Byron is indeed psychic.

In moments of calm, such as when Byron is eating some gnocchi in the corner or having a cigarette in the alley despite having perfect skin (What does he know?), he will occasionally look off into the distance, then apathetically deliver a premonition. During my first month, when I didn't even think he knew my name, Byron told me to switch shifts with my coworker Sara, and that next day Sara's identical twin with whom she had been separated at birth came in for lunch and they were reunited. Try getting *that* out of a lifetime's worth of quality health insurance.

When I ask Byron point-blank if he's psychic, he just shrugs and sips some espresso from a tiny espresso cup, but he also doesn't deny it, which adds to the mounting evidence for my belief. Last month I was taking the trash out, and Byron calmly stepped outside and told me to move a few feet to the left, then an A/C unit fell from a window two stories above where I had been standing. When I looked up to thank Byron for saving my life, he was already back inside getting invited to the Italian villa of a regular.

He also predicted COVID. Like the whole thing, beat for beat.

Now if I'm ever in a situation where I need to state my primary care doctor, I just give the restaurant number and say to ask for Byron because if there's anything that needs to be known about my health, I'm sure Byron knows it. By that same token, I no longer require insurance since clairvoyance allows me to take a preventative approach to my wellness. If I'm on the path to illness, Byron will warn me and gently steer me away from it. When I tried to confirm this with him, he raised an eyebrow, then cleared a table of six without creating even a decibel of sound.

TIP:
Keep a framed photo of your bank account on your desk so you can remember what you're doing this for.

If Byron ever confided in me any detail of his life, I would be honored. If he asked to move in with me, I'd take the couch. If he started a cult, I wouldn't join because I really do want to give this sculpting thing an honest shot, but I would support him emotionally. For the most part, Byron doesn't speak to me at all, but that's all right. He's not my therapist, he's my psychic coworker who I have because I can't afford Cobra.

But Byron, if I do have any psychological problems coming down the pipe, please do let me know.

Productivity Advice from Boomer Dad

"Wake up and try not to have a heart attack."

My Work Doesn't Define Me. It's Just Where I Spend the Majority of My Life

And I spend the rest of it in my under-decorated and generally neglected apartment, which doesn't define me either! It's just a place that I rent with the majority of my income.

A EULOGY FOR THE GIRLBOSS, FOUND DEAD IN HER MINIMALIST GIRLBOFFICE

By Freddie Shanel

Dearly beloved, we are gathered here today to mourn the loss of our Girlboss, Sandra Graham, who regrettably passed away last week in her minimalist millennial pink girlboffice.

I share your sadness and disbelief that what you thought was Sandra assuming the "Shavasana" corpse pose as she does every day for an hour was actually just a corpse. Nonetheless, I am sure this is how Sandra would have wanted to go out: on the morning of an investors' meeting after a quarter of downward-trending sales.

What is there to say about Sandra that the 2017 *Forbes* profile, "The She-E-O Who Isn't Afraid to Show Her Claws," hasn't already said? Indeed, she was "a trailblazer," a "modern mogul," and, by international standards, a "labor regulations violator," but she was so much more than that. She was also a Rockstar Badass who broke the glass ceiling and leaned the fuck in, all the way to her untimely death.

Sandra ruled with an iron fist and kitten heels, which you may recognize as the opening sentence of the 2018 *Forbes* re-profile, "Iron Fist and Kitten Heels: Do Sandra Graham's Workers *Deserve* Money?" But as we remember her, let's not discuss the superficial things, just as she forbade us from discussing our grievances, hours, or salaries, and subtly sexually harassed a young female intern.

Her policy of "radical transparency" meant we never needed to guess what she was thinking. It also meant several of us could see her choke on a zucchini through the glass walls of her office, because that's what radical transparency is all about.

Yes, I tried to give Sandra the Heimlich, but she insisted—as she did with every other aspect of her life—on doing it herself. This proved difficult given that there was no furniture to use for leverage in her minimalist girlboffice, and the Le Corbusier couch in the reception area was too squishy. Indeed, one pays for independence with one's life. Sandra said this often, generally to employees who were considering leaving.

I know Sandra's passing has left us confused and, frankly, unsettled, the same way I felt any time I looked at the single painting on her wall, an all-red canvas with one black dot that she said represented "feminine oppression."

But if Sandra Graham was one thing, she was our boss. She proved to all her doubters that a woman *could* run a company and that company *would* still have a lot of the same HR complaints as any other. And that is a woman's right.

Sandra never let those naysayers get her down, even though it was kind of hard to determine what was sexism and what was nuanced critique of someone who climbed the corporate ladder without ever asking, "Why?" and "For whom?"

Sure, she may not have paid us a living wage . . . That's actually it. I thought something nice might come to me in the moment, but sadly that was not the case.

Sandra lived an honest-ish life and did honest work: ensuring no substances would ever again be tested on animals that are cute. Thanks to her, 75 percent of the cosmetics industry now only tests on animals who are ugly, because as Sandra said, "Honestly, what do they have to lose?" *That's* what I call impact.

How do we measure the value of a life? In IPOs? In male board members who describe her as "a feisty one"? In the number of magazine covers where she's holding a gavel for some reason? I say, let's do the last one. I encourage everyone here not to remember Sandra as she was—kind of aloof and unreachable—but as she wished to be: super rich.

I'm sure I speak for everyone here when I say none of us could have seen this coming, even though we technically did see it happen. I, for one, assumed she would bite the dust on the company trip to Turks and Caicos last summer, or perhaps be crushed by the glass ceiling she installed by hand "to serve as a metaphor." This tragic event certainly rivals the succulent accident that killed her nemesis girlboss, Patricia Watkins. I'm sure Sandra's up there smiling, knowing that even in death, she did it better.

So tonight, in this similarly minimalist church, we raise our glasses to you, Sandra. I trust the Good Lord will welcome you at his Gate, and I hope this is one door you also shut behind you. May you get to meet all your greatest heroes: Marie Antoinette, the fictional character Harvey Specter from *Suits*, and every woman who has ever run a bank. Hear, hear!

Productivity Advice from Boomer Dad

"Save for retirement by putting away a little bit of your paycheck every month, and patiently wait for your grandson to win the Golden Ticket."

WHY I'M PRIORITIZING MY CAREER OVER FINDING A BETTER CAREER

by Brandon Follick

I've always taken pride in the fact that I'm a responsible worker who acts seriously and puts my career first. Breaking larger business objectives into small, manageable tasks makes me feel like I truly accomplish something at the end of the day. That's why I'll never let misdirections or the unshakable urge that there's something better out there and I should find a more fulfilling career get in the way of my career, because I'm just that career-focused.

Losing sight of your real priorities in favor of temporary comfort and security can make your daily work a total killjoy, if it's not the right job for you. And nothing sounds more dreadful to me than finding such little fulfillment in your job that you learn how to autopilot your way through the day just to stay sane. Trust me, I've been doing it for years. But as much as I love the concept of finding a totally different career that feels mindful and engaging, but I'm just super busy right now with my career, so those things (joy, fulfillment) will just have to wait.

As much as I love having an upwardly mobile career, life really is about balance. But if I were to rank where I want to put my focus, obviously my career comes first because that's the thing I'm used to doing. Behind that are both my personal life and relationship with myself tied for dead last because I've never invested in knowing myself outside of my career before and that sounds scary to me.

There's also no way to measure how successful I'm doing in those less-important aspects of my life because there's no supervisor delivering my performance review, so honestly, what's the point?

I remember reading an article recently that showed people who stayed at their current jobs receive a lower pay increase than those who switch to a new job, but I'm too serious of a person to hop from job to job because I keep finding better opportunities. Anyway, there are lots of trade-offs that come with the salary increase, like learning new software and programs, challenges that push me to become a more resilient person, and enjoying life for the first time since my jobless childhood. I just learned how to use our coffee maker! Imagine I go off and work somewhere that only has an espresso machine. I'm just way too busy in my current role to even think about that kind of stuff, and for me? Being busy is enough.

Society builds a trap that makes you fall into a career that demands so much of you that you become unable to put your focus on anything else in life. Would I love to one day either quit or work less so that I can invest in my creative hobbies or travel or even start a family? Absolutely! But I can't even think about a life beyond preparing slide decks for a living until I finish this very important slide deck. This might be the one that could change everything!

After all these years I've put into brand marketing for pharmaceuticals, it's almost impossible to imagine myself in any other career. I mean, let's say I conjure up the energy to apply for other opportunities, take several interviews, and get a job elsewhere. Then what? I would be so behind on my work, put human resources through the whole rigmarole of recruiting, interviewing people then finding someone who actually wants the job, then finally hiring them to fill my position and replace me? I feel so guilty just thinking about it! Plus, I just take my career way more seriously than that.

Like any career-minded individual, I work so hard every day that I come home too exhausted to even cook, let alone job-hunt! God, can you imagine? Like any sane person with a good job that only meets my most basic needs and nothing more, I know the best option here is to just suck it up, continue doing the job I've learned that I'm best suited for, and let my fantasies for a better career (and subsequent better life) stay exactly that—fantasies. Anyway, I'm talking too much—gotta get back to work!

HOW WORKING FROM HOME GAVE ME THE FREEDOM TO NEVER NOT BE AT WORK

The pandemic fundamentally changed our culture's relationship to work. Before COVID-19, most office workers simply accepted a five-day office workweek as the way things were done, but as lockdown forced us into our homes, this long-held norm was finally pushed into question. Now office work is possible again, but I, for one, will always cherish how working from home has given me the freedom to never, ever, not be at work.

Before the pandemic, I spent so much time simply getting to and from my job. I had to wake up early, make myself breakfast, and commute all the way to my office. Now, as soon as I open my eyes in the morning, hello! I'm at work!

There's no arriving, and there's no leaving!

My life used to be so compartmentalized—go to work for work, go to the gym to watch TV on an elliptical—but now, I finally have the gift of fluidity in my day. If I want to make myself a healthy lunch from scratch, I could probably do that? And if I don't meet my goals by end of day, I can just keep working into the night. Time is a never-ending expanse with no meaningful divisions!

Remote work also allows me to take better care of myself. In the past, if I was sick, I had to stay home and take a "sick day" to not infect my coworkers. But now, I'm staying home anyway, so I can work right through my illness, all the way to a mysterious secondary infection. Chicken noodle soup with a side of spreadsheets? That's much more healing than resting all day while worrying about how I'm falling behind. I'm finally free! And on my fifth round of antibiotics!

And it's not just my apartment that's now my office; it's the whole world! Just recently, I took an *amazing* and restorative trip to Kyoto without having to take a single day off work. Because of the time difference, I had to work all night and sleep most of the day, but my hotel had really good coffee and I got to experience the cultural phenomenon of having fish for breakfast, even though it was more like my dinner, *and* I got to travel with my boyfriend, even though it was more like he was mad at me for being asleep all day.

Ultimately, I love my new life where every surface of my four-hundred-square-foot studio apartment is my desk. If you're putting work and life on opposite sides of a scale, you'll never find a perfect balance, but if you throw them together like leftover stew in a giant Ziploc bag then the scale will pierce the bag and there will be stew everywhere . . . . . Sorry, my body is still used to being asleep while the sun's out from Kyoto, and I sort of lost track of the thread there.

Here's to the ultimate freedom!

MAN CLAIMING WOMEN WERE HAPPIER WHEN THEY DIDN'T HAVE TO WORK SO CLOSE TO BEING ONTO SOMETHING

In an attempt to advocate for traditional gender roles, Thomas Reindt accidentally almost made a valid critique of pink-washed capitalism this past week at dinner.

"Are you really telling me that women are happier now that they're expected to work high-stress jobs with demanding hours?" said Reindt, who, unwittingly, has a point there. "These are jobs that were designed for men so that a single-income household could thrive while a woman took care of the children and home."

Remarkably, Reindt is dead-right that assimilationist feminism that puts pressure on women to perform labor on both sides of the previously gender-segregated, patriarchal framework does not necessarily make women happier. However, he is wrong that this is due to "biology and hormones."

"Someone has to take care of children," Reindt continued. "And that work is either going to fall on an already overworked mom, or the kids are just going to be raised by some nanny."

While employing a nanny is not wrong, Reindt is so close to making some compelling points about the fact that women perform a disproportionate amount of domestic duties even when they are employed outside the home, and the economic advancement of white women in professional fields often relies on the undervalued domestic labor of women of color.

Sources are sure this was probably what he was getting at if he just mulled it over a bit more.

"What exactly is liberating about being expected to work eighty hours a week?" says Reindt. "Is this what equality looks like? Women being the same as men?"

Feminist scholar Dr. Rebeca Wade Jackson weighed in on Reindt's statements.

"I think he's really onto something with the idea that women are set up to fail by being forced to compete with men in positions that privilege men specifically," Dr. Jackson says. "What we need to see is a radical restructuring of the workspace and the nuclear family so that people of all genders have flexibility and access to more community-based child rearing.

"I don't agree with Thomas's position that women pumping breast milk at work is an abomination, in his words. But if his conclusion is that we should have more paid parental leave, then we're totally on the same page—even though I'm not exactly loving his whole deal right now."

While Reindt allegedly believes that parental leave should not be necessary at all because mothers should stay home with their children, he is steadfast that full-time jobs should not be hoisted onto women.

"No one should be forced down a path that doesn't fit them," Reindt says. "That's why all women should be mothers and all men should work."

So, so close!

Tradlife? This Woman Is Straight

Chapter 2

Your "Side Hustle"

"Never don't be making money, even when you aren't."—Bob Ross

In our culture, we value individualism and self-improvement above all else.[18] Interestingly enough, the origin of the word "improvement" is actually the Anglo-Norman French word *"emprower,"* which means "to profit." So how do you improve yourself when you're not on the clock? By taking that time and using it to turn a *profit*, bitch! And that is why more people than ever have chosen a side hustle as their preferred after-work hobby. Whether it's driving an Uber, running an Etsy store, or defrauding millions of people through a pump-and-dump cryptocurrency scam, the side hustle is that little gig that pulls in extra dough, but on *your* schedule. And how do you execute this life hack? Instead of using your free time for rest or your dreams or holding your loved ones close, you use it to do a little more work. If you're thinking, "Working for money—that sounds an awful lot like a job," then you have great reading comprehension. Your side hustle should be "SAT tutor"! Or if teenagers scare you, try something more low-key, like selling clean urine on the black market.[19]

Anyway, if you Google "side hustle," you'll find plenty of news stories about people who turned their blog or lizard birthday party planning service into a six- or seven-figure income business, but this isn't the reality of the side hustle for everybody. Much like having a "side piece" in addition to a main relationship, it's something that Don Draper would probably make look cool, but will leave you utterly exhausted and wondering why it wasn't as sexy as it looked on prestige television. In our current rise-and-grind climate, working multiple gigs is something you may just have to do to stay relevant and/or remain housed. The stakes might be different in either

---

18   Okay, we value rich white women with selective Black features above all else, but this is a close second.
19   This is what we consider "passive income."

situation, but one thing connects them both: the feeling that our day job just isn't paying enough for us to live the lives we want, or the lives our parents had. Why do you think Rihanna and Kylie Jenner needed to sell all that makeup?

Maximize Post Engagement so You Can Turn Your Life Into a Little Business

Only Mark Zuckerberg is profiting financially, but if you break a thousand likes you might feel loved!

Reasons for a Side Hustle:

- Get paid to do your hobbies!

- A way to finally pay back the witch that cursed you.

- To finally buy back that car you sold as a "joke."

- A way to show your friends that you have the self-discipline not to call a mysterious old woman a "dumb bitch" and then challenge her to "curse you."

- To retire early (82.5 years old).

- To surround yourself with other driven young hustlers, then offer them up to the witch in return for freedom from the curse.

- Extra cash for dinners out!

Fortunately, there are so many ways to get your side hustle on. You can turn your car into an energy drink ad. Oh, you don't have a car? What about a bike? No? Okay, you could just get the Red Bull decal tattooed directly on your body. Then you could probably go viral for being that Red Bull walking ad person and turn your side hustle into your personal brand! But we're getting ahead of ourselves, because your side hustle isn't just a job, it's a *mindset*. And like all mindsets, if it's not shaping every aspect of your being, you ain't doing it right! It's called "having a personal brand," sweaty!

For now, just start by making sure you charge your sister for every time you hang out with your niece, and then use that money to buy an apartment and rent out the futon in your living room. It doesn't matter if you're "family" and she "didn't even ask you to babysit." Time is money, and that little girl should know that owning property is the key to wealth. Bonus points if you set up an Etsy shop for her macaroni jewelry! Hustle, baby, hustle!

WOW! THIS COLLEGE FOOTBALL PLAYER IS GETTING PAID IN EXPOSURE TO A TBI

Talk about inspiring! After years of hard work and personal sacrifice growing up in a low-income community, eighteen-year-old defensive tackle Tyler Clemens just accepted a full ride to Penn State University on a football scholarship. And while Tyler is not receiving any kind of salary to join the Division I football program, he will be paid in exposure to NFL scouts and several traumatic brain injuries before the end of his college football career.

"I'm so excited to take my football career to the next level," Tyler told us after his announcement. "I'm ready to train hard, play hard, and hopefully get paid for it in four years."

We'll see about that, Tyler!

"I worked so hard for Tyler to get into college, and now that he's got a scholarship, I'm over the moon," says Tyler's mother, Linda. "I'm gonna be in the front row every game cheering for Tyler to get his head crushed for the cost of a state-school education."

Tyler is excited to concuss at a higher level on this D1 football team, and dreams of getting even bigger, more damaging TBIs on national television someday in the NFL.

"I really want to work hard and go pro," says Tyler. "I know I can get there if I can just learn to take some hits from bigger guys on the field. Then it'll all be worth it."

Tyler is also excited about the recent change in rules that allow college players to accept sponsorships, which was previously prohibited to preserve the "amateur" nature of the sport.

"I'm definitely open to getting a sponsor," Tyler said. "Right now, I'm being courted by an energy drink. And it's cool 'cause they'll pay me in energy drinks. Man, I love football."

In spite of this incredible opportunity, many doctors warn of getting paid in this kind of exposure so early in life.

"Repeated head injuries have a close link to CTE, a life-altering degeneration of the brain leading to dementia, depression, and mental illness later in life," says neurologist Dr. Tom Jacobs. "And it's terrifying that players like Tyler are going to get this kind of unprecedented exposure without even attaining the salary of a professional football player."

But the peace of mind that comes with "protecting your brain" doesn't even come close to the thrill of getting to play football for thousands of people in one of the most competitive leagues in the nation.

"I really hope I can go all the way with my football career," adds Tyler. "I don't think I was meant to have a regular job. It looks like it rots your brain from the inside out."

#Hustle Inspo:
When Steve Jobs was designing the first Apple computer, he tied his dick to it so if he wanted to take a break, he would have to tear off his own penis (he only did this once).

HOW TO TURN YOUR HOME FOR WAYWARD CHILDREN INTO A CONTENT HOUSE

Running a home for wayward children can be a thankless business, but it doesn't have to be! If you've taken waifs, ne'er-do-wells, orphans, and urchins alike off of the street and brought them into your manor for young unfortunates, then it's about time you found a way to monetize them. That's where content houses come in: a content house is a mansion with no furniture where a bunch of TikTok-famous teens live together so they can make viral videos all day in the hopes of being able to pay for college, earn a living, or have a Dunkin' Donuts drink named after them. Here's how to finally make this draining yet tax-exempt setup worth your while by turning your home for deeply troubled, wayward children into a content house.

Make them learn dances.

Dance can be a beautiful form of self-expression and bodily alignment, which may help troubled juveniles connect with their best selves, but this really isn't about that—this is about those adorable little rascals going viral on TikTok. Therapeutic interpretive dances are out, and perfectly choreographed and executed group routines are in! Don't be afraid to really drill these fuckers hard.

It's not like you're making them brush the floor with a toothbrush. What else would they be doing? Pickpocketing? Sowing mischief into the streets? Better that they be learning the top trending dances created by a Black tween, then made famous by a white teen, then executed by a group of mangy children in an overgrown manor for nothing but clout!

Invest in ring lights.

The children might complain when it's gruel for dinner again, but you don't just have twelve little British mouths to feed, you also have twelve sickly, pallid little British faces to light! Agatha's Story Time about being the sole survivor of a mysterious fire in her former orphanage just isn't going to "pop" unless she's brightly enveloped by a state-of-the-art LED ring light on an extendable tripod that goes low enough to capture these freakishly short, malnourished (thanks gruel!) little children.

Create a fair reward system.

These wayward tikes may never have experienced unconditional love from a parental figure, and it's important that they still don't. You're not running a charity here; you're running a content house. The "British orphan" brand is compelling, but they still need to remember that they're up against Los Angelino teens with rich dad resources and model mom genes. Incentivize these unruly youths with rewards like "a blanket" or "a rich couple is coming to pick a child" (a rich couple coming to a home for wayward children? Lol, yeah right). This incredibly fair system will reward the children that are willing to work hard and/or sabotage the others. If you find some true narcissists in the mix, you may even have the opportunity to upgrade from content house to reality TV!

So get the content churning with a TikTok of a wayward child churning butter, and before you know it, your little shelter will be a content house of the highest rank. And just like all other content houses, you'll have viewers thinking, "Where are their parents??"

SHOULD YOUR POLYCULE INCORPORATE FOR TAX PURPOSES?

So your polycule, a connected network of non-monogamous people in a loving relationship together, has solidified into a committed unit—congrats! You've formed a beautiful relationship with people who want to explore a life together. But have you discussed the tax implications with your team? If you've entered into a committed relationship and are worried, like most people, about the collective tax burden, here's how to know if your polycule should form a corporation:

Have an open, honest discussion about becoming a business entity.

Ask the most important question to your loved ones: "What are we?" and start figuring out what to name your LLC from there.

Get a CPA who understands your business goals.

You got together because you enjoyed having sex and spending time with one another. But a good accountant will understand the most important part of polyamory: trying to limit your tax burden. And knowing who gets the "big" bedroom on the weekends.

Are they willing to outsource?

Once life gets busy, you may want to outsource key roles in the relationship to keep the business on track. Are you willing to hire contractors to fill in as the person who initiates group meetings, or the charming trickster who never does the dishes but always gets away with it?

Be open to outside investors.

You never know—if you raise enough capital, your polycule might end up being a unicorn!

Don't be afraid to acquire other fast-growing polycules in a hostile takeover.

There's tons of competition out there, and your best bet is to devour them before they kill you first. Remember: There can only be one!

Marriage may not be an option, but that doesn't mean that you can't turn your sexy, free-loving little home into a ruthless corporate entity. Here's to loving freely!

#Hustle Inspo: In her busy position as First Lady, Eleanor Roosevelt was known to take any stimulant lying around to stay awake. You name it—skippies, black beauties, jiffies, truckers' fuel, a crushed-up Ritalin from her time-traveling drug dealer. She'd do it all and be first one in the office the next morning.

DO YOU HAVE ADHD OR IS THE PACE OF LATE CAPITALISM LITERALLY IMPOSSIBLE WITHOUT STIMULANTS?

By Lizzie Logan

Before you begin an ADHD treatment regimen that includes stimulants like Adderall or Ritalin, it's worth asking yourself if the symptoms you're experiencing come from a chronic neurological condition or have been brought on by the incessant and untenable pace of productivity under capitalism, requiring you to take low-grade meth just to get through the day. The two experiences are strikingly similar!

Usually diagnosed in childhood, Attention Deficit Hyperactivity Disorder can manifest in a number of behaviors. Some of the most common are aggression, boredom, anxiety, forgetfulness, and difficulty focusing. An economy in which workers are expected to simultaneously juggle dozens of tasks and are increasingly in competition with one another for an ever-smaller share of the marketplace can also make a person aggressive, bored, anxious, forgetful, and unable to focus. There may be no way to know for sure what's causing your problem, as you'll likely never retire.

Taking certain amphetamines has been shown to help people with ADHD focus for longer periods of time. The same pills also help people without job security stay up all night to meet quotas and survive yet another round of layoffs. Do you need a doctor or a union? It can be hard to tell.

In the mid-2010s, Wall Street experienced a small rash of seizures and deaths among junior bankers who had used various stimulants to work punishing hours, sometimes going as long as three days without sleeping. If the pressure on these well-compensated high-achievers necessitated medication, the stress on workers who need to take extra shifts just to make rent is surely just as taxing. By making employees think they can't hack it without powerful, habit-forming drugs, corporate America impresses its shareholders and keeps the masses from recognizing the need for systemic change. So do you have a problem with your brain? Or do you just have a lack of paid time off, universal healthcare, and a healthy working culture? Maybe you could ask your doctor (she won't know, but she *will* charge extra for the "mental health assessment").

Consider that for most of history, the human brain has only needed to compute tasks like "pick berry" and "walk to well" from the hours of sunup to sundown, so your disinterest in checking your email at 11 p.m. might actually mean that your mind is working exactly as designed.

Questions used in making a diagnosis of ADHD include:

"How often do you have difficulty keeping your attention when you are doing boring or repetitive work?"

"How often do you have difficulty unwinding and relaxing when you have time to yourself?"

"How often do you interrupt others when they are busy?"

With a "hustle" mentality, workers are expected to leverage their every waking hour for maximum profitability. One could certainly understand a person being unable to focus, relax, or wait for a colleague to be free in those circumstances. Either way, it's time to pop a pill!

ADHD, ADD, and other neurological conditions are real, and deserve a response other than "stop working so hard." In some, they require treatment using prescription medicine and behavioral therapy. That's nothing to be ashamed of! It's equally true that we'd probably all be a lot better off if we got outside once a day to take a walk, but there's no money to be made in relaxing strolls, so the market will never allow it. We just need to find a way for taking walks to involve the collection of our data so that we can sell it in order to take more walks. Or just become a walkfluencer? Either way, it's gonna take some Adderall to plan that all out.

If you believe you are suffering from ADHD, labor exploitation, or both, consult with an expert to find the solution that's right for you. It'll probably end up being stimulants no matter what because humans are just not built to do all the thousands of stressful micro-jobs required of us today, but thankfully, there are pharmaceutical remedies that will allow us to keep making a little money for ourselves and a lot of money for others, especially the pharmaceutical companies. Behold, the circle of life!

How to Take On Freelance Work to Make Spare Cash for That Vacation You Won't Have Time for Because of All That Freelance Work

Step 1: Take on a freelance job to tuck away some extra cash. Drive an Uber, wait tables—the sky's the limit!

Step 2: Plan that vacation! The Maldives, Bali . . . you can finally afford it with all that extra cash!

Step 3: Think about what a waste of money it would be to fly to Bali—you'd have to spend like three weeks there to even justify the travel. Anyway, you'd have to quit your freelance gig, which means no more fancy vacations! Anyway, this extra cash could go toward an early retirement, the likes of which still seem incredibly vague, yet compelling enough to keep endlessly delaying any sort of gratification in life. Maybe you can go to Bali then?

Step 4: Get back to work!

HOW TO EARN PASSIVE-AGGRESSIVE INCOME

So you want to earn a little extra income on the side? That's so cute. No, really, it's adorable that you would be so desperate to want to try something like that. You really want advice on how to do this? Aw, sweetheart . . . we're *kind* of busy writing a book here . . . did you not notice, or . . . ? No, no—it's fine. Yeah, no, we're happy to put aside our extremely busy and important jobs that feed our families (who don't appreciate us!) to share some ways that you too can make your own passive-aggressive income. Just keep on reading if you really want to know, or just flip the page if you think we don't have anything to offer you . . .

Make an E-Course About How Nobody Really Listens to You.

E-courses are an amazing way to make extra cash on a one-time effort, so why not use this opportunity to build a three-hour online course about why nobody really listens or cares about you? Or don't. Why start listening to us now, right? You certainly didn't when we said you looked "tired."

Start a GoFundMe Called "Keeping Score of Who My Real Friends Are."

Asking your contacts for money in this way might lack subtlety but will be very effective for letting you know who to furiously unfriend when they don't give you at least fifty dollars. Plus, you look like you could use it?

Rent Out Half of Your Space, Then Let Them Know How Hard It Is to Be a Landlord.

This can earn you thousands of dollars a month and give you an opportunity to complain about doing basic tasks you are legally required to do, like taking out the trash or making sure the heat works. They can just enjoy living the luxurious, worry-free life of a renter while you tell them how hard it is to pay for a plumber until they agree they should be paying more in rent. Just remember to sound disappointed when you don't give them their security deposit back because the floor looks "walked on." Aw, you're really doing it now! It's funny, you don't seem like someone who picks things up fast.

Invest in a High-Yield Savings Bond You Will Use to Reward Those Who Are Loyal.

You may not be thinking of this now, but buying a twenty- or thirty-year bond will be the perfect way to earn a reliable return and also reward the one grandchild who didn't betray you all those years, even when the rest of the family has blocked your phone number because of "boundaries." It's sad that they're so spoiled, but we're praying for them.

Become a Financial Dominatrix Where They Pay You to Tell Them How Hard It Is Being You.

There has to be at least one rich guy out there who will do this. And if you find him without telling us, we won't get mad but we will definitely be wondering why you'd do that to us when this was actually our idea . . .

Look, we're tired, and if you ask us more questions, it's really going to hurt us, both physically and emotionally. Good luck, sweetheart!

#Hustle Inspo:
Lions don't listen to the opinions of sheep, so if all your loved ones are like, "We're really worried about you; you're acting insane," that's a sign to keep going.

OH NO! THIS WOMAN BUILT HER BRAND AROUND MAKING ANTI-WORK MEMES AND NOW SHE HAS TO KEEP MAKING THEM

Twenty-eight-year-old Cassandra White made waves when her irreverent meme account critical of the modern work environment @dankfuckworkmemes blew up to over a million followers. But things started getting complicated when she realized she has to keep making them because it's kind of her job now.

Better get back to work, Cassandra! The people demand more!

"This started as a fun side thing so that my friends and I could just have a laugh about how shitty our jobs were," says Cassandra, who quit her unfulfilling full-time gig two weeks ago. "I still fully believe in the mission, and people need to understand how they're being exploited. But now I'm kind of running out of ways to explain that work sucks? Also big brands keep stealing my work and using it as free advertising and I feel totally out of ideas, which makes me feel pretty shitty."

Fans absolutely adore her acerbic take on modern-day struggles with long hours, low wages, demanding bosses, and the meritocracy myth, but a few followers are concerned about the quality and volume of the content she puts out.

"I fucking love that account. It points out all the bullshit that our whole lives are based upon," says one fan. "But some of the memes are getting kind of repetitive? I just feel like she could put more effort into the content I'm consuming for free. I've told her this in the comments several times."

"It's something I really want to share, but I'm starting to get emotionally drained, under too much pressure, and financially exploited by the platforms I post on," added Cassandra. "Anyway, I gotta go make a TikTok dance about why labor relations are fundamentally broken in the United States because the algorithm demands it."

While Cassandra still believes in her mission, she feels conflicted about taking time off from the project for some self-reflection.

"If you stop posting, they'll forget about you, and if they forget about me, what will I have left?" Cassandra added. "This series of blurry Garfield memes is the most important thing I have in my life right now. Anyway, I gotta go repost another one where Garfield is the capitalist and the lasagna is low-wage workers."

We hope you keep up, Cassandra! Your fans are waiting!

HOW TO STOP WORRYING ABOUT CLIMATE CHANGE BY PROFITING OFF OF IT

By Madison Dillard

You might be worried about the growing effects of climate change, and for very good reason. After decades of warnings, we're finally at the point where we're seeing the ramifications right in front of us. With so many powerful forces willing to destroy the planet, you might find yourself feeling helpless about what to do or where to turn to. We don't really have any good advice on how to fix it at all, but here's a step-by-step guide to stop worrying about it by profiting off this disastrous ecological event instead!

Get involved in pro-apocalypse industries.

Boats

A rising tide lifts all boats, so why not enjoy the (devastatingly) high seas by investing in boats? With the sea level continuing to rise from all of Earth's ice caps melting, boats are going to be high in demand from the coastlines of Kansas to the rocky beach cliffs of Colorado. Bad news for pretty much everyone on Earth, but good news for you if you invested in the boat industry early. Get that money!

Owning water

Scientists say the world's water demand is projected to grow an astronomical amount by 2050, which means that hoarding fresh water now will have an astronomical return when we hit ecological collapse! So when our Current World looks more like Waterworld, make sure you get a cut of those sweet water profits as early as you can. Too bleak? Try renting it out instead! Getting it back will be the hardest part.

Alaskan Air Conditioning Services

What's a better way to secure the market than selling the first air conditioning systems in the formerly freezing U.S. state known as Alaska? Since we all already know what's coming, get ahead of the curve by spearheading the A/C industry when it gets as hot as Florida there (Florida will, of course, no longer exist). Stop stressing, and you will thank us later!

Real estate on Mars

With the Earth going to shit, one thing's for sure, and that's that people will be absolutely *gagging* to live on Mars. In the past, the Earth becoming uninhabitable may have stressed you out, but once you're making *trillions* in real estate, you'll be like, "Earth *who*?" Make that shmoney!

Support Politicians That Support You Making Money
Financial support

Money goes a long way—you obviously know that by now or else you wouldn't be trying to make so much of it off of the destruction of Earth! So take the edge off your concerns that millions will be left homeless and make sure to fund the candidates who continue to claim that climate change is a myth. Remember: You're just doing this to profit from the inevitable. You don't have to believe them! This one will be extra good for your mental health.

Online activism

Another great tool to use to ensure that the Earth won't be protected is to become an activist online for the causes you now believe in, like "Climate change is a myth," and "Caring about the environment is kind of dumb and bad when you really think about it." This will help people get on your side, or at least be too confused to do anything while you're enjoying your new boat. It's not your fault no one listened to Al Gore. Why should you take the fall?

Your vote

Kidding of course! This doesn't matter.

When you're making so much money off of the destruction of the planet, there's going to be some pushback. That's why one of the most important things to remember during your business ventures is to deny, deny, deny. People are going to tell you that profiting off of climate change is wrong, and even though you know that it is, tell them that they don't have their facts straight, and also that they're trying to spread the gay agenda or something. This always works! Saving the planet is, objectively, very gay.

It's so depressing and hopeless to feel like the bad guys are winning, but what if that was your home team? You'll be sleeping like a baby when you choose not to give a shit about future generations and make a buttload of money in this shitty new world. You're welcome, future millionaire!

#Hustle Inspo:
This robot factory worker doesn't take pee breaks.
What's your excuse?

ECONOMISTS WORRY NOT ENOUGH MILLENNIALS CAN AFFORD TO GENTRIFY A NEIGHBORHOOD

By Brandon Follick

Since the onset of globalization and the Internet Age, being able to live your best life in the city has been a part of the millennial's American Dream.

However, a team of researchers from the Economic Policy Institute recently published some troubling data that found most millennials are no longer able to keep up with the rising prices required to gentrify neighborhoods. Naturally, this is causing widespread fear and panic to stakeholders in the urban residential market whose entire existence relies on being able to reach deep into the young generation's pockets to ensure housing is unaffordable for those who have lived in neighborhoods for decades and barely manageable for wealthier displacers, at best.

"While many Gen X and older millennials had the privilege of ushering in the first wave of higher household incomes in poor urban areas, we've seen that younger folk haven't been quite as able to afford housing that unroots the longtime occupants and even entire multigenerational homes as easily," shared lead researcher Eric Johnson. "We're worried the many new condos being built today might remain empty, or worse, will turn into affordable housing."

Most millennials are renters, and nearly half of people between the ages of twenty-three and thirty-four years old are rent-burdened, meaning at least 30 percent of their incomes goes to gentrifying neighborhoods. After the regular costs of food, healthcare, student loan debt, and software coding bootcamps, there's not much disposable income leftover to throw into a savings account for future events like the housing market fucking itself up again.

Tragically, the gentrification affordability gap has widened even more during the pandemic. A number of factors combined to make this possible, including the desire to live alone after spending too much time with family, roommates, or now-exes; the halted production pipeline of new rental units due to labor and materials shortages; the end of federal assistance like rent moratoriums; and the influx of remote workers who can pitstop in the city before finding a better ZIP code whose residents they can outcompete.

These unplanned events conspired together to amplify the preexisting issue that millennials could barely even afford to culturally destroy a neighborhood to begin with.

"This market is unsustainable for me personally if we can't keep the millennials here," shared community developer Jerome Parker, 38, on the verge of anxious breakdown. "Without young people here as consumers for the hip hop yoga studios or Japanese-style, White-owned Izakayas, my entire investment portfolio is fucked. I knew features like adding a collagen coffee gastropub in one of my apartment buildings was a risk, but this is all so unfair to me. The government needs to step up and help us little guys out."

Indeed, the government has done little to nothing when it comes to updating zoning laws or offering loan programs that protect these socioeconomic movers and shakers.

"My heart goes out to these young new residents who came from families that could probably once afford to buy a Great Lake," shared longtime resident Veronica Holley, 74, who has lived in the neighborhood for fifty-eight years. "I guess they'll just have to go back to Ohio. Oh, well."

A study from the Pew Research Center found that, when it comes to financially planning for long-term gentrification, the overwhelming majority of millennials financially plan to either be saved by a Hail Mary federal policy or learn someday that they have been written into a random will.

"I'm just hoping one of my grandparents is secretly rich and is so humble that they don't want us to know until an executor administers their estate and hands me a fat check," confessed relatively new resident Clare Jennings, 26. "I feel like I might have some stocks in an old tech startup I worked at, but I should hold onto it in case something happens, like I need to find an apartment in another unaffordable part of the city or have to go to the emergency room even just once."

#Hustle Inspo:
The only difference
between you and
Kylie Jenner—actually
there are a lot of differences,
but they're all your fault.

The Pros and Cons of Having Goals

Pros:

- People will tell you you're "killing it" constantly!

- You'll smoke less weed!

- Less time on phone!

- Something to wake up for!

- You may accomplish them!

Cons:

- People will expect you to be "killing it" now ☺

- You'll smoke less weed ☺

- Less time on phone ☺

- Something to wake up for ☺

- You may have to accomplish them ☺

HOW COLLEGE DEADLINES HELPED ME LEARN TO MORE EFFECTIVELY MANAGE MY LIES

A formal education can help you learn to think critically and expansively, but even more importantly, it prepares you to enter the job market with skills you need to excel in your field. College is a major investment, which for many includes accruing significant debt with the hope that it will all pay off down the road. For me, the staggering workload at my competitive institution of higher learning was invaluable, not just for the content of the work, but for the way it forced me to learn how to effectively manage my lies across many jobs and other roles in life.

College, much like the real-world workplace, is sink or swim. When you've got a twenty-page research paper due at the end of the week, a physics lab, finals, a response paper for a book you haven't started, and a group presentation *en español*, it's vital that you sit down, grab a planner, and start spinning a web of lies that will help you just kinda push everything down the line, or evade your responsibilities altogether.

When you get to the real world, you can't just say your grandma died for the fifth time. You need to lie better than that.

A lot of people will ask, "What's even the point of going to college if you're not going to do the work?" and the answer is: It will prepare you to have a real job where you also don't do the work, but now you're getting paid for it! It will also prepare you to lie in order to take time off because there is literally no other avenue to do so.

Of course, managing your lies requires social skills, foresight, quick thinking, and adaptability. Remember: Your sick aunt can need a ride to her doctor's appointments as much as once per semester (you can try for different aunts, but as you add them on, they'll pack less of a punch). And once you secure an actual job, she can only die once, period.

A dead relative is an example of an emotional lie, which is great for garnering sympathy and lowering expectations for the quality of your output. I learned this during an oral exam for a gender studies course, in which I defined Judith Butler's theory of gender performance as "wearing bows and stuff." I then added, "My grandfather performed the gender of man before he died last week." I got a B-.

I applied this same logic when I told my boss that I couldn't digitize eighty client files because eighty was the age my godmother (who practically raised me) had hoped to live to. You don't get grades in adult life, but he just said, "Okay, whatever," and offloaded the task to my coworker Marcus. I could not be operating at this level without my Ivy League education.

Requesting extensions to observe made-up Russian-Orthodox holidays, calling in sick, and hiring a Task Rabbit to call in the occasional bomb threat may just seem like ways of pushing tasks down the road and making things worse for the future you, but if you manage your lies expertly, you will never have to face this reality. Also, people will learn you're unreliable and ask for less from you so long as keeping you is cheaper than training a new hire. Happy lying!

#Hustle Inspo:
If you don't defend billionaires, who will defend you when you are a billionaire?

—*Anonymous*

WHAT TO DO IF YOU MADE THE APOCALYPSE YOUR WHOLE PERSONALITY BUT NOW EVERYBODY'S DOING IT

By William Miller, nineteenth-century apocalypse predictor

Lots of people are talking about the end of the world being near these days, and I can relate: Over a century ago, I spent my life warning that God would consume the Earth once and for all on a precise day in 1843. Hundreds of thousands of people followed me and awaited my predictions. Even though the apocalypse did not come to pass, I had put so much time into making the apocalypse my "thing" that I felt like I had to keep it going—you know, for my fans.

Back then, making the apocalypse your whole deal was interesting and unique, and you could build a huge following of frightened wheat farmers if you just yelled loudly enough on top of a soapbox. But nowadays, it seems like *everyone* is doing it, which makes the whole endeavor a lot less special than it used to be and honestly kind of a waste of time. If this sounds like you, here's how to redirect your time and energy onto something else now that everyone is yelling about the End Times.

Understand the trends.

If this were a hundred years ago and you decided to devote your life to warning of the coming apocalypse, I'd say, go for it! Get attuned to the local vibe and build your story around whatever they're freaked out about the most. But nowadays, everybody's got their own predictions, whether it's nuclear war, climate change, the sun burning up and dying, or even "the mainstream media"—and it's like, okay, there is definitely something there, but isn't it kind of boring when *everybody* is in their own little apocalypse information silos and nobody can agree on just one? It's so hard to cut through all the noise now, even when you're *sure* that God will send a plague of locusts down to Earth in 2026. If you're trying to get attention, pivot to something else. It's like, yeah, the world is ending—we all get it! People are so brazen to think that *my* apocalypse prediction (the second coming of Christ) was silly, but *their* apocalypse (communism?) will so surely happen. Have some humility. You're all very late on this trend.

Don't be afraid to admit when you're wrong.

Look—thinking the world is ending is a natural human reaction to living in confusing, changing times, so you're not crazy if you devote your entire life to yelling about it in the town square or in a nuclear holocaust subreddit. Whether you've bought $30,000 worth of canned food for the impending civil war or just think that the world will be subsumed by the ocean in 2050, just remember that hey, both can happen! But if you're more worried about being smugly correct about your prediction than doing something about it, you've fallen into the same trap that I did. Don't do it! I doubled-down on bad math (I got my Jewish and Gregorian calendars all mixed up) because it would have been *really embarrassing to be wrong.*

Find another hobby.

When God didn't end up unleashing the seven plagues upon the Earth like He promised (What the Hell?), it felt like my entire reality had been shaken to its core. I left myself with nothing else to fall back on, and yet, the world kept on going, regardless. When you accept that the world may not be in flames as you had once hoped, this is a good opportunity to acknowledge that the apocalypse had a meaningful place in your life—honor that! And then maybe find something else to do, like cross-stitch, or, I don't know, get into running? Just try not to tour around the country by horse, gathering thousands of followers to heed your warnings that ultimately results in a fringe religion that people are like, technically fine with, but still think is kind of, you know, weird? People get really, really sad when you tell them the world is going to end and then it doesn't. Emotionally it's, like, intense.

Remember how insignificant we all are.

Some people like to think that the end of the world is going to happen in their lifetime, maybe because they cannot accept that they are not that important and don't have a divine role in the story of the universe (oops, me!!). But as I'm still coming to accept, the world isn't ending, it's just *changing*, and we'll still have to go on and live in it. What if this is just the way things are? Where will you focus your energy then? Which leads me to my last point . . .

DON'T start a new religion.

As tempting as this is, don't! You'll just end up as another podcast, just like the rest of the doomsday cults, murderers, and doomsday cult murderers.

There are plenty of reasons to think that the world is ending, but I promise: People thought the same thing one hundred years ago, five hundred years ago, and before then. Do your best to make the world a better place and accept that change is inevitable and doesn't mean the apocalypse is near. Anyway, back to my doomsday bunker in Hell!

How to Find the Perfect Work/Work Balance

It can be hard to find the right balance in life between work, your other work, and the work that you need to do to do all that work. But don't worry—you're not alone! Over 90 percent of people feel like they don't have enough time for work when they aren't working. If you're looking for a healthier work/work balance, here are some tips:

1. **Block out your time** between work and work so you can do your hardest work at your most productive, and easier work when you're asleep.
2. **Learn to disconnect.** It's hard for us to let go and just work sometimes, but try lighting a candle, running a bath, and bringing your laptop into that bath with you. But be careful—that's a work computer!
3. **Set boundaries.** Sometimes, you have to be honest and limit your workload so that you can spend more time with your work and work. After all, you're not defined by your work—you're defined by your work! Now that's something to ~~think~~ work about!

Finding your work/work balance is different for everyone, but we hope you get a little closer to creating a little more free time for all that work. Good work!

IS YOUR INNER MONOLOGUE ON-BRAND? HERE'S HOW TO CHECK

By *Justine Jung*

It goes without saying in this day and age: Your personal brand is everything. From your clothing, online presence, lifestyle choices, Twitter prose style, where you live, who you date, and precisely how you fuck are things you're likely already monitoring very closely. But what about your thoughts? While you may think the most private parts of your consciousness should not have to be filtered through the criteria of your personal brand, you'd be wrong, and if anybody discovered your off-brand thoughts, it would *not* be good for you. So, if you're not sure if your stream of consciousness is aligned with your brand, here are some questions you can ask yourself:

Does this inner monologue match the overall vibe of your previous content?

Do a deep dive into your own brand history and compare it to your last rambling stream of consciousness before drifting off to sleep. Is your mind's whimsical ramblings in line to the brand you'd like to project? If not, fix it! Consistency is key!

Would you tweet the thought you're thinking? If not, why are you thinking it?

For any given thought that passes your mind, ask yourself: Is this something I would commit to my timeline? Have I tweeted something similar in the past? If so, what were the analytics like? Taking a data-driven approach can help you work out what kind of personal musings should be reinforced as a central part of your brand, or which should be cycled out as a one-off bit. And if this isn't a thought you would necessarily send out as a tweet, put that thought away!

Ask yourself: What would your followers think about your thoughts?

Let's say we could somehow record the flow of narration coming from your psyche when you're going about your day and upload it to Spotify and play it out loud for a focus group of tasteful peers in their twenties to thirties. Would they use keywords like "fresh," "dynamic," and "unexpected but relatable"? If so, keep up the great work! But if they use phrases like "muddled," "neurotic and not in a chic way," or "this podcast fucking sucks," try again. You're probably off-brand! Quick! Find some better thoughts!

Even activity that takes place in the deep recesses of your psyche is a reflection of who you are as an individual, for others to reward and/or punish. This inner life is also your greatest resource and should be managed and commodified for your personal gain. All it takes is mindfulness, self-control, and authenticity. Go forth, and happy thinking and/or brand-building!

HOW TO #GRIND WHEN YOUR #SIDEHUSTLE IS #CHRONICILLNESS

What's up, chronic illness sufferers! If you think the #grind isn't for you just because you have long COVID, PCOS, clinical depression, or another devastating combination of illnesses, you're wrong, bitch! In this beautiful country, everyone has an equal opportunity to spend every waking minute striving to get money. Just because you can't #getoutofbed right now, doesn't mean you can't do the same. Here's how to maintain that #grindset (a mindset of nonstop grinding) when your main side hustle is . . . being unwell and trying not to make it into a whole "thing"!

Treat your lack of sleep as pure #grind.

Do you have a chronic illness that leaves you awake for half the night? Well look at you, you absolute #grind #hustle #bossbitch! Let people know you're wide-awake at 3 a.m. by posting a blurry selfie of you checking stocks on your laptop while you look intimidatingly unrested. People will respect you!!

Reframe any situation as #grindset.

Whether you're struck with an almost perpetual fatigue or just a constant, indescribable pain, reframe that situation by reminding your coworkers that, "Bitch, I'm making money from my bed!" Your coworkers might be like, "Are you okay?" But that's just the kind of negativity you don't need in your life. Ignoring the haters is your other full-time job!

The #grind is all about the #struggle, at which you are technically thriving.

Whether it's rheumatoid arthritis or an autoimmune disorder, the #grind is all about enduring the #struggle. And bitch, who is better at struggling than you? Pat yourself on the back and buy yourself a very nice car. Can't afford one? Just put on sunglasses and jump in the first one you can find. You've done it! You're #grinding!

Just because you haven't set up multiple streams of passive income or bought a duplex and rented out the other side, doesn't mean what you're doing isn't hard. Now get out there and find a #naturopath that understands your specific hormonal fluctuations and dietary needs!

Congratulations! You Are Reading a Book

Okay, wow. You're not only reading a book, but you're well on your way to *finishing* one. Wait until your friends hear about this. At this point, you could probably post it as "finished" on your mostly fabricated Goodreads profile. Don't worry, we won't snitch but we won't forget, either. Congratulations!

1. Embrace feeling vulnerable! It will help distract from all the people who are laughing at you for being such a loser.
2. Replace your sense of pride with feeling even more incompetent than you previously thought possible.
3. Remember that receiving help is a requirement of this embarrassing little life you've carved out for yourself.
4. Know that you can reciprocate help to others in the future, solely to regain your sense of superiority.

SHIFTING BRANDS: SHOULD YOU CHANGE YOUR BABY TO FIT YOUR FEED OR CHANGE YOUR FEED TO FIT YOUR BABY?

Although you may drive yourself crazy trying to get every part of your life ready for a new baby, the factor of the matter is, nothing can *truly* prepare you for the reality of having a child. But one of the hardest adjustments of motherhood is the utter vibe shift it will cause across your social media platforms. How does your baby fit into your feed? Well, that's a personal question, and the answer lies within you. With that said, you can use the pool of wisdom from mamas before you to help determine if you should change your baby to fit your feed or change your feed to fit your baby.

If you're really on your A-game, then you gradually adapted your Instagram aesthetic over the course of your pregnancy to fit your baby, like carefully decorating a nursery with gold and neutrals instead of having your partner hastily assemble a crib in the corner of your bedroom while you went into labor. But not everyone is so able to think ahead. What if your personal brand was "alt-grunge" before baby, and your Instagram was all used bookshops, dive bar bathroom selfies, and new tattoo reveals? The good news is, there are multiple ways to approach this conundrum. For example, you could post a pic of your partner perusing a used bookstore while casually carrying your baby, to show that your infant hasn't disrupted your primary vibes but is more of a seamlessly integrated accessory.

Of course, if you're going to change your baby to fit your feed, you also need to keep a close eye on its aesthetic. You've had a beige color scheme going for longer than this boob-feeder has been alive, so you're not going to just 'gram baby in the hideous giraffe onesie your sister got them and fuck your grid to hell. Find a complementary color and slap it on to slowly incorporate this baby into the visual theme you call "motherhood."

On the other hand, if you prefer a sharp rebrand to make your feed fit your baby, that's also on the table. After all, parenthood is gonna basically be your whole thing for the next eighteen years, so you might as well get something out of it. Just remember: the first few months after baby is born, you'll be getting tons of "congratulations" likes. Those numbers are not indicative of a sustainable brand trajectory. Random pics of your wrinkly baby's face do not an online identity make. You'll need to go full homemade baby food, funny *and* adorable videos, and heartfelt "keep reading" captions about your difficulty with latching if you want to keep this up.

At the end of the day, whether you change your feed to fit your baby or change your baby to fit your feed is a deeply personal decision with no one right answer. And if you want to avoid the choice altogether, you can just post pictures of your baby with an emoji over its face like you're a celebrity, which everyone will be united in hating the most!

HOW TO FIT FIGURING OUT YOUR GENDER IDENTITY INTO AN EIGHTY-HOUR WORKWEEK

Whether you've landed a competitive position like advertising or law, or you're just working multiple jobs to make ends meet, navigating a shifting gender identity can take a huge amount of emotional energy and time that you simply might not have. If you're questioning whether or not you're actually cis but also extremely busy, then take a look at this sample day to see how to incorporate your personally vital gender questioning into your eighty-hour workweek:

7:30 a.m. Wake up from that weird dream where one of your secondary sex characteristics fell off your body. Quick, get in the shower!

7:40 a.m. Take a shower, then let a non-verbal fear wash over you as you edge toward considering the impact actually paying attention to your nascent transness would have on your life as you casually check your email.

8:15 a.m. Use your commute to catch up on some transphobic news!

9:00 a.m. Dissociate from your body so you can do whatever it is you do on your little computer for four hours.

1:00 p.m. Lunch time! Take a break from it all and eat a sandwich while trying various Instagram filters that make you feel all kinds of weird.

1:30 p.m. Final stretch! Just six more hours of meetings before you can head home and research gender-affirming therapists.

7:31 p.m. Oops! Your boss would actually love if you could finish his job before you head out. Steven already said he'd stay late to work on it with you. Fucking Steven. He always calls you "bro" or "girlie"—whichever of these irks you on the deepest level of your soul that you're yet to unpack! Anyway, be a team player?

9:30 p.m. Arrive home in a fugue state, unsure how you got there. Eat the pad thai you ordered while watching that fantasy show on HBO Max about characters who develop as people over time.

11:00 p.m. (optional) Smoke weed.

11:04 p.m. Experience a wave of panic about the fact that you are probably trans and are going to need to eventually do something about that.

11:05 p.m. Tell yourself it's just the weed or being stressed and tired.

11:06 p.m. Brush your teeth while looking way too hard at yourself in the mirror.

11:15 p.m. Decide that you're actually cis and everything is fine. Anyway, you've got some work emails to answer!

12:00 a.m. Hit the hay, slugger! Any unresolved thoughts will bleed seamlessly into your unconscious, then you'll wake up fresh and ready to cope with them!

7:30 a.m. Today's the day! Oh, God, Steven texted "hey [bro/girlie], down to come in early today to iron out kinks in presi? i'm already at the office!"

7:31 a.m. Resolve to think about this tomorrow!

Chapter 3

Your "Wellness"

Have you tried meditation? —God

Humans have existed for millions of years, and yet nobody can agree on a precise definition of what "wellness" even means. Before capitalism, it might have just been "living to age thirty," but now? It can mean a million things depending on your culture, your class, your upbringing, and your willingness to listen to an uncertified chiropractor/acupuncturist on YouTube. But one thing seems clear: You can be happy while physically unwell, but you can't really be truly well if you're chronically unhappy.

But since your physical wellness can contribute to being unhappy, the whole thing becomes *just* vague and confusing enough to build a whole industry and a few religions[20] around it.

What we do know is that people will spend billions of dollars trying to achieve this idea that can only vaguely be defined as "fixing everything wrong in life with bath." The majority of us have been exploited to varying degrees, worked to exhaustion, then left so tired that all we want are the sweet yum yums[21] they sell to us, all while an underfunded public health sector tells us to get more rest and stop buying our lil' num nums because they're "bad for us." Thanks, public health sector! You're just one "lose weight" away from being our toxic mom!

And the reason it wasn't so easy to see was that it didn't happen overnight: Thousands of years ago, humanity worked exactly enough to have shelter, eat, and stay warm. Everything was literally perfect and there were no problems plaguing society.[22] But then, someone else decided if they just work a little harder, they could maybe kill an extra giant rodent/dinosaur and take the rest of the day off, while the sucker family in the cave next door toiled on

---

20 See also: MLMs, cults, your divorced friend who did ayahuasca once.
21 We're specifically talking about microplastics.
22 We consulted several anthropologists about this.

picking nuts and berries.[23] The system learned to exploit our desires to have some additional security by making it less and less achievable with every generation—at some point, it went from something that was kind of true to an outright myth, like the idea of American exceptionalism, or that Avril Lavigne died in 2006 and was replaced by an impostor: it's really more of a feeling than a fact.

And the irony is that you can only be *truly* productive if you are relatively "well." In other words, cultivating one's own wellness is yet another full-time job needed to optimally perform your full-time job and your other full-time job,[24] which is why successful people are usually born rich and in a calming yuzu bath, and successful people who aren't born rich often find themselves fried and burnt out without an exit strategy or safety net. Can we dial down the capitalism a touch for the sake of our little bodies, or would that stress out the corporations too much?[25]

Do you need to buy expensive products and services to become "well"? Probably not, but you do need some kind of free time and at least one (1) leafy vegetable per week, which is why most people just resort to just buying the products and services. Wellness can also allow you to live your life with a sense of happiness and fulfillment, but why would anybody waste it on that?

Yes! This Woman Resists Toxic Positivity by Having Clinical Depression

---

23 Several cultures found an easy solution to this problem, but we're talking about the origins of the one that didn't.

24 See also: Your side hustle.

25 Corporations are people too, and we must respect their opinions.

Maslow's Hierarchy of Needs

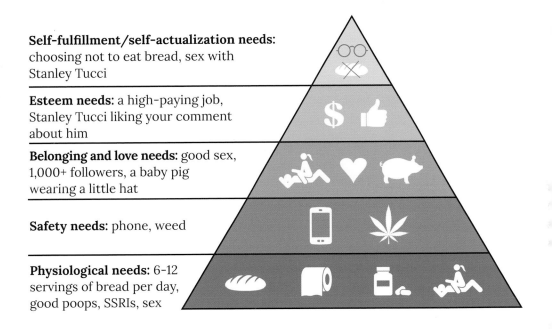

Self-fulfillment/self-actualization needs: choosing not to eat bread, sex with Stanley Tucci

Esteem needs: a high-paying job, Stanley Tucci liking your comment about him

Belonging and love needs: good sex, 1,000+ followers, a baby pig wearing a little hat

Safety needs: phone, weed

Physiological needs: 6-12 servings of bread per day, good poops, SSRIs, sex

IS THERE SOMETHING WRONG WITH YOU, OR DOES EVERYONE FEEL THIS WAY, OR IS THERE SOMETHING WRONG WITH THE FACT THAT EVERYONE FEELS THIS WAY?

Are you burnt out? At the end of your rope? Considering ditching everything for a Masters in Philosophy or maybe a conch piercing? Well, maybe there's something seriously wrong with you. Then again, it's also possible that everyone feels this way and you're totally not alone! Or is there actually something deeply, profoundly wrong with the fact that everyone feels this way all the time? These are complicated questions, but you can find all the answers with this self-guided quiz:

Can you sit in a chair looking at a screen for eight hours a day?

1. No! It makes me feel insane. I want to take a walk. I want to feel the wind against my face. I want to live.
2. No one can! Get some blue light glasses and suck it up. We're all in this together, girlie!
3. From the time we are children, the public school system molds us into obedient subjects while penalizing and pathologizing behavior that challenges this subjection. We are all victims of the ideological forces of the state.

Do you feel guilty for no reason when you have free time?

1. Yes. I always have a looming sense that there's something I should be doing even if I don't know what.
2. Join the club! A great way around this is to never not be busy— just a tip.
3. This feeling of guilt is a result of the idea that your productivity is indicative of your worth. This fundamentally degrades the integrity and sanctity of human life, which is sort of bad, actually.

How does the existential threat of climate crisis strike you?

1. Not well.
2. This is a stressor for everyone (except people who don't believe climate change is real. Lucky!!). You kind of just have to push these feelings down and keep doing your life. Good luck!
3. To fully acknowledge the devastation of a Sixth Extinction is basically to go insane and be unable to function in society. Plus, your government and Big Oil have been gaslighting you about climate change your entire life, so it probably makes you feel pretty crazy already! We're all going through this, but at the same time, it's sort of like we shouldn't be.

TIP:
Take a short nap by looking at your phone, but horizontally.

Do you have a bit of a stomachache all the time?

1. For sure.
2. Who doesn't!? Just switch to oat milk and keep trying your best.
3. Actually, feeling physically unwell from early adolescence onward should not be normalized.

Results:

All answers: The good news is, the results are in and they're simple! No matter what you answered, yes there's something wrong with you, yes everyone feels this way, and yes there's something wrong with the fact that everyone feels this way. Basically, society is not good. Is this news to you? At least you're doing your part (reading a little book!).

Anti-Capitalist Hero? This Woman is Asleep

COTTAGECORE-APPROVED WAYS TO TREAT AN STI

If you're not familiar with cottagecore, it's the Tumblr-originated, nostalgic, pastoral aesthetic that has taken the internet by storm. Cottagecore emphasizes slowing down and being one with a little cottage: hand-baked pies cooling on a windowsill, washed-out picnic blankets, oversized sweaters, and rustic prairie dresses. Cottagecore also harkens back to the days before penicillin, so if you're looking to cure a recently contracted venereal disease without modern medicine (whether it's because you want to stay authentic or don't have health insurance) then try these absolutely cottagecore-approved ways to treat an STI to stay consistent with your brand.

Eat honey.

Pure raw honey already has a total cottagecore vibe, perfect for mixing into a cup of tea and supporting bees! Does buying honey support bees? Does it do the opposite? Whatever, this is about your sexually transmitted infection, not bees. Raw honey boasts complex antibacterial properties, which is great for your fucked-up pussy. Should you eat it? Should you put it on your vulva? We don't really know. Please keep in mind, this is not medical advice; it's more of a vibe!

Take echinacea.

Taken medicinally, echinacea has been shown to boost the immune system and fight infections like the chlamydia you got from Jonah, the neighboring farmhand, (previously known as the Entrepreneur at Self-Employed you met on Hinge). Like most medicine that fits a CC aesthetic and doesn't require a trip to CVS, it apparently "doesn't really work" and you "need antibiotics." But that's just the city-slicking haters talking. What's a little painful urination in exchange for pretending you live in an overgrown cottage while you put some dried echinacea extract into your Nutribullet? This is so much better than civilization.

Practice abstinence.

This is a more preventative than treatment-oriented approach, but abstinence remains the best way to avoid an STI, and it's totally cottagecore-approved! What could be more bucolic than sitting in your little kitchen, making a mincemeat pie from scratch, and not being fucked by anyone? It's giving farmcore, it's giving frolicking through a meadow, it's giving a white frock that symbolizes virginity, honey! And if you think it's problematic for us to appropriate queer AAVE, maybe consider that the romanticization of Western agricultural life is also pretty problematic, as is encouraging abstinence! Pick your battles, fae bae!

Patiently wait for the sweet release of death.

What could possibly be more cottagecore than a long, slow death from a treatable infection? Wasting away in the country is as chic as it gets, and dying from a lack of access to healthcare is as Americana as it gets. Taylor Swift and Lana Del Rey will both be dying from envy, but you won't get to see because you'll be dead from death.

TIP: Put a crystal in your vagina. Then another. Just a few more. You're so close to beating the world record for number of crystals in a vagina!

So take care of your sexual health and your aesthetic health with these cottagecore-approved treatment plans. And if you're looking for a change in style, consider a Dark Academia abortion!

NOT GETTING ENOUGH SLEEP IS LITERALLY KILLING YOU. HERE'S HOW TO KEEP DOING IT.

Many Americans report not getting adequate sleep, which is one of the main causes of life-shortening diseases like diabetes, heart disease, and depression. In other words, staying up later, working longer hours, and watching *Law & Order* reruns at 3 a.m. is literally killing us. But it's not like you're just going to stop, right? So here's how to keep on getting that sweet, sweet lack of sleep long into not-so-old age:

Maximize screen time.

Stare at every screen you own until the blue light makes it impossible for your body to produce its own melatonin. You'll be killing a pedestrian with your car in no time!

Change your perspective on sleep being "good."

That's just a rumor started by Big Mattress and people who want to live long and healthy lives. It's entirely subjective!!

Dwell on your biggest regrets.

Do you need to construct an elaborate list of things "you could have done differently with your ex? "Sleep time" (the time where you lay in bed awake for hours) is best for this!

TIP:
If you have a fever and are vomiting, take a "sick day" and just relax in bed! #selfcarehack

Watch all eleven seasons of *Frasier*.

We dare you to turn off your TV mid–Season 3 on this '90s classic! You fucking can't!

Have children!

They're good for this one thing specifically!

Drink lots of water.

You'll be too busy pissing to sleep! This is another reason hydration is overrated, but in this instance, it will serve you.

Sleeping might be the easiest thing we can do to live longer, healthier lives, but that sort of thing just isn't for everybody. Now get out there and answer some work emails at 4 a.m.!

HOW TO CONTRIBUTE TO A HEALTH SAVINGS ACCOUNT WHEN YOUR DREAM IS TO LIVE IN A GORGEOUS EUROPEAN TUBERCULOSIS SANATORIUM

A Health Savings Account (or HSA) is a type of savings account that allows you to set aside untaxed income for qualified medical expenses. You can use your HSA debit card for deductibles, copayments, and even everyday pharmaceutical purchases. Contributing to an HSA is a smart choice for your wallet and your health, but it can be difficult to make that choice when your real dream is to live in a gorgeous, nineteenth-century tuberculosis sanatorium for the rest of your fleeting days, coughing up blood here and there as a kindly nurse looks upon you in anguish. Use these tips to make a practical choice instead of a romantic one that involves reading poetry in the countryside, wearing a lot of loose-fitting clothing, then dying in a hot and tragic manner.

Pick a Health Savings program that meets your needs.

Numerous banks offer HSA programs, with each touting their own unique benefits. Do a little research to find out which might be right for you. Of course, there is no HSA option that will grant you residency in the hallowed halls of a mountainside sanatorium in the Italian, French, or Swiss countryside, where patients enjoyed "sun baths" and healthful walks through tree-lined gardens during their convalescence. The American healthcare system could never, and also tuberculosis now has a cure, unfortunately.

Think practically about tax-deferred savings.

Contributing a cut of each paycheck in order to pay future medical bills is nothing if not a practical choice. Living out the rest of your days in a fresh air sanitorium, taking strolls with a parasol, or lying on a chaise lounge on a breezy terrace is neither practical nor possible, but wouldn't it be great? The Romantic poet Lord Byron once said, "I should like, I think, to die of consumption . . . because then the women would all say, 'See that poor Byron—how interesting he looks in dying!'" And it's like, we hear you, Lord Byron! This definitely sounds more interesting than taking one of your five state-mandated sick days and lying on your couch using your HSA to get Capsule to deliver you some extra-strength Tylenol, but such is your boring life!

Stay healthy.

The beauty of an HSA is that it's there when you need it, but the best care is preventative care. Take care of yourself by eating a balanced diet and getting plenty of rest—even though you have no time to do either of those things, and both of them would be provided for you in a gorgeous sanatorium where you could lie in bed outside, waited on hand and foot, surrounded by your other, terminally tubercular friends. An outside bed!! What is more deluxe than that? What is more romantic? Literally nothing. Your life sucks compared to this and you just have to accept that and keep doing your best.

Perhaps it's problematic that tuberculosis was considered a "fashionable" disease that enhanced one's creativity and skinniness even though it had devastating effects on otherwise-healthy young people. And perhaps romanticizing sanatoriums, which were only available to the upper class to begin with, is also problematic. After all, coughing up blood and then dying is not something you *really* want, and contributing to an HSA is an undeniably superior approach to managing your health and finances. Maybe what you really want isn't to live out your days in a European sanatorium, but more just, like, a vacation? Anyway, good luck trying to pull *that* off!

SHOULD YOU TRY SSRIS OR KEEP MENTAL ILLNESS YOUR BRAND ON TWITTER?

SSRIs can be a life-changing and life-saving form of psychiatric care, but that doesn't mean they're for everyone. For instance, what if your voice on Twitter heavily relies on having an untreated mental illness? It's a personal decision (unless you make a poll for your followers), but we can get you started with some pros and cons to consider before deciding either way.

SSRIs

- Can alleviate symptoms of anxiety and depression

- May improve your relationships

- May make you feel more stable

- Could leave you feeling numb to certain experiences in the world

- Yummy yummy serotonin☺

Mentally Ill on Main

- Can give a voice to others living with mental illness or just people who feel sad sometimes

- May improve your follower count

- May make your brand (of debilitating depression and/or anxiety) more stable

- Can give you just enough outside emotional support to keep being mentally ill on Twitter

TIP:
To reduce screen time, destroy your phone at least one hour before bedtime.

TIP:
Check the color
of your pee, just
for the fun of it.
Is it good? Nice!

HOW I RESIST GRIND CULTURE BY SETTING ASIDE THIRTY MINUTES OF EACH DAY TO JUST IMAGINE OSCAR ISAAC MAKING ME MARINARA SAUCE

Hustle culture, also known as "grind culture," is an insidious trend that valorizes those who never stop working or "grinding." The rise-and-grind mindset promotes the ceaseless generation of money or ideas and otherwise contributing to a growth-oriented capitalist economy. When we start to conflate our worth as people with the worth we generate, we devalue the sanctity of human life. We forget that we *are* enough just for existing, and that the creeping anxiety of always feeling like there's something else we should be doing is just another way our culture brainwashes us into overworking and over-consuming. Luckily, there are manageable yet radical ways we can subvert these hegemonic forces by reclaiming our time and our minds. That's why I practice resistance by setting aside thirty minutes of each day where I just sit with my eyes closed and imagine Oscar Isaac making me delicious marinara in a galley kitchen.

Grind culture mentality is also a highway to total burnout. A lot of people try to avoid it with self-care, but my practice runs deeper than that. You see, I'm trying to fundamentally rattle the paradigm of how I move through the world. That's why in my fantasy, the marinara sauce Oscar Isaac makes for me is homemade and slow-cooked. He starts by sautéing onions over a low, steady heat in a gorgeous Le Creuset dutch oven (yes, my fantasy involves expensive, name-brand cookware. We live in a society—sue me!).

You might be wondering why a Latino actor is making me marinara sauce. Well, that's all explained by Oscar himself. He tells me that though he's Guatemalan and Cuban, due to the Anglicization of his name, olive skin, and sculptural nose, he's often been cast as Jewish or Italian, and as a result has learned about these respective cuisines. Then he offers if I'd like to sketch a charcoal portrait of him in profile while he hand-smashes the tomatoes, and I gratefully accept.

He's wearing a tank top. It is thin.

My daily ritual of imagining Oscar Isaac preparing me fresh tomato sauce contributes absolutely nothing to the world, and I like it that way.

In it, I sit on the countertop as he stands by the stove stirring the simmering sauce, and we make happy and easy conversation while I try not to stare too hard at his forearms. Then he walks over and stands between my parted knees, having me taste the sauce off of a big, hard wooden spoon. But that's enough of that because I'm not trying to arouse you. That would be productive and this activity is not.

A lot of people would say that my practice of sitting and fantasizing about Óscar Isaac Hernández Estrada making me sauce is a radical act of daily resistance, praxis, "the work." And all of these people would be correct; you should listen to them. Imagining a world that's different from the one you exist in is actually one of the hardest parts of resistance, and for many people that looks like imagining a world without prisons, without police, without the violent subjugation of the working class. Those exercises are totally valid, and I wouldn't discourage anyone from doing them, if their minds are not yet free enough to simply close their eyes and see a crystal-clear image of the *Inside Llewyn Davis* star breaking a light sweat while he dices celery or winking at them while he puts some salted butter into the simmering sauce. There's a guitar in the background, but it isn't played. The only "grinding" will be done by Oscar himself (freshly ground pepper on top of my pasta).

So no matter what I have going on—late bills, late work assignments, late period—I never prioritize these concerns ahead of my thirty minutes of sauce time. My friend imagines being on the back of a jetski with Ethan Hawke for a full hour every day, which I think is a psychotic fantasy, but I commend her hustle! I mean . . . her stillness and fortitude. Here's to disrupting the #grind and getting one step closer to seeing if I can cum hands-free!

> **TIP:**
> Develop a loyal follower base! You'll need them someday when you have a medical emergency that insurance won't cover.

IS IT CHRONIC FATIGUE SYNDROME OR GOD'S PUNISHMENT FOR EATING FROM THE TREE OF KNOWLEDGE?

Do you feel tired all the time, like sleep is never fully restful for you? Even before we faced a life-altering pandemic, more people were experiencing unexplainable lack of energy that doctors were unable to diagnose. If you have unexplainable fatigue, weakness, or digestive issues, it's possible you could have Chronic Fatigue Syndrome (ME/CFS). Then again, that feeling of never being fully rested could just be God's punishment for all of humanity for just being alive. Doctors are only beginning to understand the many complex issues that cause so many people to be fatigued with no clear explanation. So is it a legitimate medical condition, or just the ultimate retribution from a vengeful Old Testament god? Let's find out:

Did you recover from a viral illness?

Chronic fatigue has been linked to viral illnesses like Epstein-Barr or COVID-19. If you recovered from a virus before symptoms set in, this might be what's causing your never-ending malaise. However, if this is something that's just kind of persisted as long as you can remember, this might just be God smiting you for the sins of your ancestors. If that's the case, don't be so hard on yourself! You only get one cursed life!

Do you have a hormonal imbalance?

Many people with chronic fatigue report having hormonal imbalances that may be correlated with CFS. It can be difficult to find the right doctor willing to take you seriously and look into this, so if she just dismisses you and tells you it's all in your head, you can always blame God.

Have you experienced any physical or emotional trauma?

If you've recently had either a significant emotional trauma or physical accident occur, trauma has been known to spur symptoms of CFS. If the only trauma you've experienced is just the pain of being alive, that one's most likely on ol' Eve for just *needing* to eat an apple 'cause a snake told her to. Who listens to a snake about apples? When have you seen a snake eating an apple? Whatever, it's in the past (though its consequences are haunting you to this day).

Did you make God very, very angry?

Honestly, this one could go either way!

There are so many complex reasons why we're unable to fulfill the basic needs of our day, and modern medicine is finally coming closer to understanding why. Talk to your doctor about the potential autoimmune diseases you could have, and if not—repent! Repent for your sins!!

Wow! This Woman Told Her Primary Care Physician All Her Problems and He Was Like 'Yeah IDK'

The Best Uses for Coconut Oil

---

1. Hair mask

2. Get into an intense argument with your friend about whether it's safe to use as lube

3. Make popcorn with it for a subtle coconutty flavor

4. Tell your best friend that only water-based lube should be going inside your vagina

5. Moisturize!

6. Start to feel bad that you're being judgmental, but then double down because you've already solidified your position and it's too late to backtrack

7. Use to treat minor scrapes

8. Tell your best frien you hate her partner. Oh, my God. Did you really just say that?

9. Make a non-toxic insect repellent

10. Start crying because you're fighting with your best friend

11. Smash the bottle of coconut oil against your wall because it's sowing hatred and drama into your life

12. UV ray protection

13. Pick up the shards of slippery coconut oil jar glass. They are your best friends now. They are all you have

14. Natural deodorant

HOW TO COMPROMISE WITH YOUR PARENTS BY HAVING .5 CHILDREN

Millennials are having fewer children than any generation before them. But in spite of rising costs, crushing debt, and the prospect of working full-time while raising children, your parents still desperately want a grandchild or two. And can you blame them? They are super bored and need something to play with. While some people might settle on having one child instead of two or three, not all of us could afford such a luxury of raising a whole, human child. So, how do you put away the idea of getting another dog and compromise with yourself, your parents, and the constant nagging fear of dying alone? Draw some inspiration from the Old Testament and ruthless technical compromise to make sure everyone is happy! Here's how:

Let Mom and Dad know this is the most child you can afford.

You already ran the numbers: One full child would be 100 percent too much child for you to afford and offer a decent quality of life. When you factored in your shared apartment with roommates (you share a kitchen), your semi-committed partner (you share a credit card) and your combined income (you share $20k in credit card debt), you calculated you could afford exactly .48 percent of a child. Once they see this all on paper, they'll totally understand how you got there. Plus, you're rounding up because oh my God, how weird would it be to only have .48 percent of a baby? Just remember to show your work!

Ask them if they want the bottom half, the top half, or a whole baby split vertically down the middle.

Sure, lots of older folks imagined playing with a baby, or spoiling a toddler, but not everyone can afford these kinds of luxuries. You know how they could afford a three-bedroom house with a backyard on one income, but today, you and your partner can barely afford a studio on two incomes? Having babies is exactly the same—our generation just has to downsize their children a little bit! Just make sure you ask them very clearly which half they actually want, 'cause the cleanup is expensive and time-consuming.

If they squabble about "what this all means, because this sounds very disturbing," remind them that compromise requires an open mind.

When they inevitably grow "deeply concerned" about your "thinking," just remind them that they come from a very closed-minded generation and they need to loosen up a bit. Lots of people aren't having any children at all these days, and that's a viable and respectable path. And if they press further about whether this involves cutting a baby in half, having a super-small baby, or a collection of parts that would make up 50 percent of the mass of a baby, remind them that you don't owe them all the details of your birth plan—that's private!

Have a half-baby shower.

If they're still worried, remind them how nice it is to buy half as many gifts and baby supplies—more money for Grandma and Grandpa to enjoy their retirement margaritas!

Show them the closet where the creature will live.

Seriously; whatever gets them going!

Raising children is no easy task, but we all still have the freedom to throw the rules out the window and find our own solutions apart from society's rigid ways. And don't worry—when your parents see the beautiful eye of their grandchild (if that's one of the parts you're keeping), they'll fall in love immediately!

Don't Have Kids? Monetize the Idea of Having a Niece!

WHY I HIRED A DOULA AND THEN SPENT MY ENTIRE LABOR WONDERING IF SHE WAS HAVING A GOOD TIME

By Alyson D'Lando

When you discover that you're pregnant, there are countless decisions to make. Should you give birth at home or in a hospital? Medicated or unmedicated? Announce your pregnancy on social media or wait until your kid goes to college? All of this takes a lot of time, research, and unsolicited opinions to figure out, but one thing I was absolutely sure about was that I wanted a doula to support me through the pregnancy and birthing process. Mine was named Amy and she was fantastic! During my twenty-nine hours of labor, I can honestly say she was invaluable.

I cannot, however, say whether or not she had even a remotely good time because she was super hard to read.

As soon as I arrived at the hospital, Amy started creating a calm and peaceful environment. She rubbed oils on me, did light touch massage, and helped me try different positions. It really did feel like one of my best friends was in the room! But what I did not anticipate was that just like hanging out with most of my friends, I would end up spending a good deal of time wondering if she was mad at me.

What many people don't know is that doulas are extremely skilled with pain management. Through mindful breathing exercises, Amy coached me through the intensifying contractions while I struggled to keep my eyes slightly open so I could watch her facial expressions for any kind of feedback.

Another perk of hiring a doula is that they also support your partner through the birthing process. In my case this was my husband, who was great, but having Amy around allowed him to be there for me in other ways, like answering my constant texts from across the room asking if it looked like Amy was having an okay time (he says it looked like she was, but how could he really know?).

Doulas are labor experts and are there to remind you that everything you're feeling is normal. Amy had been to over six hundred births, which I originally saw as a positive, but around my ninth hour of labor, I realized that, statistically speaking, there's really no way I would even rank in her top ten favorite labors. This realization ruined the next twenty hours of my labor for me entirely.

As the doctor broke my water and I sat in a puddle of amniotic fluid vomiting from the pain, I wondered: What I could do to make Amy more comfortable? It was around this point that I attempted to tell some jokes. I was very tired by this point and I do not recommend this. That's all I really want to say about that.

TIP: Gummy vitamins fall under the vegetable category of the food pyramid.

It finally occurred to me when the doctor came back in to fist my cervix for the fifth time and tell me it was still gonna be a while: I told Amy she should totally go home. We could text her when the big show is about to start since she probably had better shit to do. But she very sweetly said, "Not only do I want
to be here, but you're paying me to be here."

That's when I realized she definitely hated me.

Around hour twenty-three I was finally able to sleep for a bit. This was hugely helpful to rebuild my stamina, but not hugely helpful in the sense that I'm almost positive Amy went outside to text all her doula friends about how she was at the dumbest labor ever and was now reconsidering her career path.

When I was fully dilated, the nurses asked how I would rate my pain, but when I asked Amy how she was doing, she just kind of smiled and gave me a thumbs-up. Is that, like, a five? Or a low seven?

As the baby's head became visible, Amy looked elated. She must be having a good time! But then I went and shit in her face, so emotionally I was pretty much back to square one.

When my baby finally came out, I put her on my chest, and wow, the clichés are true: I felt more love than I'd ever felt before! And as I laid there having my vagina sewn back together, I felt nothing but grateful. I forgot all about the pain, except for the pain of not knowing precisely how Amy was feeling and if this whole thing was really worth it for her.

I never did find out if Amy had a good time. But I guess it was a good lesson for parenthood: You won't always have the answers but you are definitely free to obsess about them until it keeps you up at night and eventually takes over your entire state of being.

To all the doulas out there, thank you for everything you do! And to my own doula Amy, I will never forget you and can you please give me a letter grade?

What is Emotional Labor?

Emotional labor: It's a phrase you've doubtless heard, and probably said, but what does it truly mean? Apparently, its definition has to do with the demand on service workers, and particularly women of color, to perform happiness and friendliness even when it is strenuous to do so at their jobs. But, like, come on! We should *all* get to use this term basically however we want, obviously. Regardless, you should have an answer prepared if someone ever asked you what it actually *means*, so here are some of our best guesses:

- When your boyfriend asks you a question

- When you're doing whatever your job is but you don't want to

- When you go grocery shopping while you're depressed, and you carefully inspect the honeycrisp apples for firmness and surface blemishes despite feeling indifferent toward the inevitability of death

- When your best friend who has been there for you through thick and thin needs to vent to you for a minute about something serious going on in their life

- When your mom asks you a question

- All doctors' forms

- Unloading the dishwasher

- When your kid asks you a question

- Introspection

- When you have to ask for your salad dressing "light, medium, or heavy" even though you know these are subjective terms, and no answer guarantees you will receive your desired amount of salad dressing

- Reading?

- Anything where you have to use a cutting board

- The expectation to remember your answers to personal security questions

- Texting your grandma "Happy birthday"

- Lingerie

- Email (sending or receiving)

- "Business casual"

- Informing your server of any allergies in your party

- Being informed of someone's allergies

- Drinking water

- Explaining what emotional labor is

DO YOU HAVE A CRUSH OR AN ILLNESS?

Nothing is more awesome and terrible than having a crush: your heart flutters, your stomach churns with butterflies, you can barely focus on work or school, and have a lump in your throat that seems to be worsening over time. Ah, romance! If you're wondering if those confusing feelings are a good, old-fashioned schoolyard crush, or actually an illness that requires acute medical care, here's how to know the difference:

Understand the cause of the swelling.

Does thinking about this person make your heart swell five sizes? You could have a serious crush on them, or you could have myocarditis, a life-threatening condition that requires immediate medical attention. Honestly, you should probably go to the hospital either way!

Examine your body's reactions to a text message.

Does your heart skip a beat when you see a text from them? Does it hurt? Sometimes a crush can be perfectly real but also reveal a dangerous underlying condition that should be examined immediately. Call 911, then text your crush that you just called 911—they might be worried about you!

Write down exactly *how* your body wants to throw up when you think of them.

Does thinking about their smile or the idea of them saying, "You're really special to me" make you want to throw up because it's so impossibly good, or are you actually just throwing up? This one is tricky—if you're not barfing, you might just not have a big enough crush, but if you *are* barfing, you could have a host of acute illnesses in addition to a perfectly normal crush on someone. Do not reach out until you have identified the cause of the barf, or the consequences could be deadly.

You're having acute pain in your left arm, chest pain, feel lightheaded, and have collapsed on the cold, hard floor.

This one still could go either way! Hoping it's just the crush!!

Knowing the root causes can help you determine if you should drop everything, be vulnerable, and put yourself out there to tell them how you really feel, or just take some ibuprofen. You can only call out of work for one of them, so choose wisely. We're praying for you!

Chart of a Man's Brain Who Feels Chill All the Time

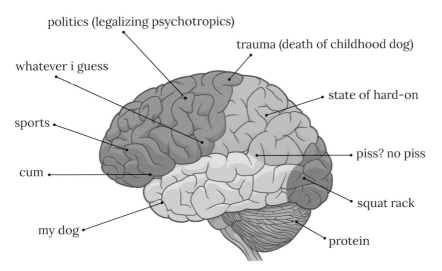

HOW TO PICK UP THE PIECES WHEN YOU FIND OUT YOUR PARTNER HAS JUST BEEN SAVING FOR RETIREMENT THIS WHOLE TIME

Many of us have been in the working world for some time now, and if you've been going along, paying down your student loans, and maybe even putting away some savings, it can be utterly devastating to find out that your chill, liberal-arts–graduating, "creative" partner has secretly been saving for retirement all this time. It's mighty convenient that she "never thought" to mention she had been "making 401k contributions" since she was twenty-three. What *else* is she hiding? If you're feeling utterly betrayed and wondering if your entire relationship has been a web of lies, here's how to deal with the fact that she's been saving for retirement behind your back this entire time:

Give yourself some time to deal with this.

Just because your partner has been living a secret life with a series of "tax-deductible IRA contributions" doesn't mean you need to immediately start doing the same. Take some time to feel your feelings before Googling what any of that means.

Remember that you technically never asked.

So the person you consider your "lover" and "best friend" has a year's salary saved for retirement and never even mentioned it, and now your entire sense of reality has slipped out from under you. Who can you even trust anymore after years of her being like "lol I'm so broke haha"? Even though you may feel like you don't know what's real anymore, remember that you technically never asked about it. This is clearly information she should have disclosed to you on the first date, but she apparently had "just assumed you were doing the same the whole time." It may be hard when you feel like you don't even know her anymore, but try to forgive her for being a cold and calculating savings sociopath.

Talk to someone who can relate.

If you're feeling isolated and alone, find someone who can relate. If you don't know anyone in this precise situation, try and talk to someone who realized their partner was living a double life and had a secret family in Ohio or something—pretty much the same energy there.

Try to salvage what's left of the relationship.

So you just learned the person you wanted to marry someday has the capacity for future planning and follow-through. We can't blame you if you want to pack up your bags and leave, but if you've invested time into this relationship, it's worth trying to understand where they're coming from and see if you can start afresh from a place of honesty and maybe also get some tips on, like, what a savings bond is or something like that. Not that their teaching you that will make up for this betrayal but . . . it's a start. Of course, if you learn that they've actually been investing in "stocks" and "options" this whole time as well, just blow the whole thing up and walk out. People who know that much about investing cannot be trusted!

It can sometimes feel like we're never doing enough as adults, and when someone close to you seems to be succeeding at it without telling you, it can be devastating to your psyche. Fortunately, there are plenty of people like you out there, so it's good to know that the ones who have a year's salary's worth of retirement funds by the time they're thirty are the *real* freaks. We'll be over here working part-time at the Metaverse Starbucks until we're ninety!

HOW TO REPARENT YOURSELF TO BECOME A HAPPIER, STRONGER MARKET ACTOR

By Justine Jung

Parents do their best to raise us well, but often by the time we reach adulthood, we come to realize we have a few blind spots in our social-emotional development and we're far from being our ideal selves. This is where reparenting comes in: By giving yourself the nourishment and support you didn't receive as a child now, you can empower yourself to be the truly fulfilled, happy player in the larger economic structure you always could have become. Here's how you can kill off your feeble, naive inner child and nourish the most resilient, hypercompetent little worker bee you have inside of you!

Assess what needs were not met when you were a child and how that affects your value proposition as a human being today.

Did you have any important needs that were neglected in your childhood? For example, was no one around to convince you to do yourself a favor and learn how to code from an early age? Or maybe you didn't have access to a parental figure who told you that studying what you love will only lead to years of student debt, and you're better off majoring in accounting or something. Whatever the case may be, take a moment to get in touch with your wounded inner child: the vulnerable little kid who wanted Mommy to raise you to respond rationally to the demands of the market. There, there. Worry not! Now, as an adult, you can begin the hard, vulnerable inner work to transform yourself into an optimally performing workhorse and start easily outcompeting these other losers—just like Dad should have done!

Try to forgive your parents' shortcomings so you can finally begin to heal.

It can be hard to accept and make peace with your parents' neglect. Did it really never occur to either of them to teach you a second language, ideally one that would be in high demand with employers, during the small window of time where your brain was actually supple enough to allow it and you had a fighting chance? At this point, no amount of Duolingo is going to do much for you, and there will always just be a giant gaping hole in the 'Skills' section of your CV. But forget all that. You deserve to feel at peace! Once you start seeing your parents as human beings with limitations and flaws, you'll start forgiving them for their wasted opportunities to make you more employable. Although, it really *would've* been nice if either of them told you how to raise seed capital for a startup idea, because reparenting really can't turn back time on that one.

Dig into your subconscious and identify your core limiting beliefs.

Did your family program you to intrinsically value spending time with loved ones, without being plagued by the opportunity cost of what else you could be doing in that precious time? Do you wrongly wish you could develop a sense of community, instead of floating around cities as an atomized individual with no real sense of roots anywhere, chasing the most financially optimal life arrangement for any given time? If so, your upbringing may have been raised with some damaging anti-market values. Without judging yourself, try to identify the limiting beliefs you carry around in your subconscious mind, and write them down as statements. Maybe you believe things like, "Attending my sister's wedding is more important to me than going to this job interview, even if they offer a 401k match," or "Being TikTok-famous would *not* be the solution to all of my problems right now," or even just, "Friendship and love, as tenuous as they're made to feel sometimes, will ultimately make me happier than my career." With enough care and attention, you can deconstruct this ideology you've internalized for so long.

Slowly begin to reprogram yourself into the happier, stronger market actor you could be.

Whatever your irrational beliefs may be, you are an adult now, and you have the ability—and, therefore, the responsibility—to examine your broken inner child's core beliefs, work through those bad boys, and see them for what they are: liabilities. Instead, start retraining yourself to firmly place your sense of worth on your bottom line. Maybe you can start beta-testing billable hours for family members who want to see you when you're busy. Identify any lingering loyalties you have to any person, place, or thing that doesn't serve you anymore. Be vigilant, and constantly ask yourself, "Am I commodifying myself ruthlessly enough?" and "Where else could I be right now, and could I be getting more than what I am right now?"

So remember, even if your parents never gave you the tools to leverage your competitive advantage to game the market logic, you still have hope. Thanks to reparenting, you no longer have the excuse of Dad not teaching you to lean in as a license for you to coast through life with lower expectations. With therapy and effort, you can reparent yourself and have total control over the outcome of your existence through a series of well-managed choices. So there's really no excuse not to become the happy, resilient, thriving market actor you always knew you could be. Talk about empowerment!

HOW I TREATED MY FEMALE PATTERN HAIR LOSS AND DEBILITATING TMJ BY SIMPLY REMOVING ALL STRESS IN MY LIFE

Female pattern baldness is the most common hair loss type in women, and after the pandemic, I found myself facing what I had never imagined: clumps of my once-thick lustrous hair falling out in clumps, despite no change in my diet or lifestyle. And adding insult to injury, my once-mild TMJ turned into a teeth-cracking, migraine-inducing nightmare. So when I finally reached out to a doctor explaining my symptoms, she ran some tests and found that everything had come back "normal." That's when she told me the fact that helped me change everything: "It must be stress."

I was like, "Oh, shit. How did I not think of this?" This was a huge turning point for me: If stress was the root cause of all my health issues, all I would have to do is stop being so stressed all the time. That's it! And so I did, and all my problems went away immediately.

Why doesn't anybody else realize how fucking easy removing every molecule of stress from your life is?!

When I finally looked at my life and realized how much stress I was under, I knew I needed to make some serious changes: So whenever I felt even the slightest pang of anxiety or stress, I simply stopped it from happening, just like my doctor suggested!

The great thing about stress is it's easy to identify and then instantly cease. It took a little time to get good at it (two weeks) but eventually I eliminated so much stress that my body has literally forgotten how to produce cortisol. Choose wellness!

Now, when a friend comes to me with complaints of psoriasis, eye twitches, or a persistent, unrelenting exhaustion, I ask them with a dead, emotionless stare: Have you tried reducing the stress in your life? Usually they say, "No, I haven't!" and then they do it immediately and everything is fixed and they thank me profusely. And I'm like, "Don't thank me, thank the incredible medical professionals who have finally identified the root cause of all our problems. I am merely a conduit for their unyielding wisdom."

Now, if only I can find a way to pay the $20,000 bill for replacing all of my teeth without remortgaging my house or using the entirety of my children's college fund, I'll be all set.

Whoops, just started grinding my teeth again!

Goals! This Woman Said 'I'll Sleep When I'm Dead,' Then She Died

An open-casket funeral was held for Ashley, during which friends and family remarked she looked great. "The puffiness from under her eyes is gone. She's really rested, moisturized, and thriving," said Ashley's boss. "Of course, I still consider her responsible for getting her shifts for this coming week covered."

HOW MACRODOSING AT WORK CAN MAXIMIZE YOUR EFFICIENCY AT SEEING GOD

Lots of people have enjoyed the benefits of microdosing psilocybin (mushrooms) at work to ease anxiety and increase creativity. But if you're looking for more efficient, effective ways to see the interconnected nature of the universe and the face of God during your workday, you might want to try macrodosing copious amounts of hallucinogens instead. Here are some of the benefits of a hero dose at 9 a.m. on a Monday:

Increased awareness.

Whether you're in the office or working from home, it will be impossible not to see the beauty in everyone you meet—including the mysterious being who whispers the Truth of the universe to you while your boss is speaking on a Zoom call. Is your boss God? No, *we're all God* (your coworker who went to Burning Man "gets it").

Improved mood.

One of the many reported benefits of doing a fuckton of drugs at work is an improved mood and increased ability to tell everyone that reality is a farce, including this thing we call "work." And when The Creature, who instills both fear and reverence inside you, shows up at your daily stand-up meeting, you will know It Is Time.

No need to wait until death.

Most people have to live an entire life before they understand the Interconnectedness of All Things, but you can get way ahead on it by answering emails while confronting a full ego death at work, years before your coworkers. Finally, you're ahead! But what is "you"? And why do you have this "social security number"? Leave everything behind! You're on your own hero's journey now!

In a system designed to make us slightly yet consistently miserable, drugs may be the only way to find joy in an environment we were never built for. Don't let that get in the way of using them to see God while on the clock and find Ultimate Awareness ahead of everyone else!

Chapter 4

Your "Free Time"

Hobbies are things that aren't phone. —Steven Hawking

Do you ever feel like you have no free time, even though you just watched six hours of *Selling Sunset* and TikTok simultaneously before passing out? According to Benjamin Franklin and your great uncle Frank,[26] *time is money.* And while they both had a point, this can be a very limiting way of framing the one fleeting life you are given.[27]

One of the sneakiest things that humans ever invented was the idea of "time," because it was a way to divide your life into things like "play," "work," "sitting on the toilet while getting paid," and "sitting on the toilet for free like some kind of idiot." What started with a well-meaning sundial that allowed some Egyptians to meet around "noonish" for lunch turned into a way for us to compartmentalize our lives so much because every second is being monetized or in the service of being monetized, leaving many to wonder if their shitting schedule is sending them into financial ruin (short answer: it depends on your industry!).

In our culture, we put a lot of weight into our scarce "free" time, which puts a lot of pressure on it to be "totally awesome" or "a vacation package to Cancún I truly regret impulse-buying"—in other words, it can be put to good use or totally squandered. But if you talked to a random dude who lived 10,000 years ago, he would probably have a hard time translating what "free time" means, or understanding that you're from the future and you're here to warn him about important things, like how franchise films are ruining cinema. Once his basic needs were met, he just got to . . . *exist.* Just kind of . . . hang out—kind of like the teenagers outside of 7-Eleven except in the beauty of nature. Now, we're probably glamorizing a nasty, brutish existence before antibiotics and

---

26 Uncle Frank has also been on a "business trip" since 1997. We hope he's doing well!
27 And Uncle Frank should know—he's definitely killed people.

edible weed, but there must be a reason why people are so much happier in nature—it forces you to be *in the moment* without worrying about whether Pete Davidson is going to space[28] or if you'll ever get a refund on that vacation after the hot tub mysteriously caught on fire.

It's also worth noting that the things that seemed frivolous and time-wasting two hundred years ago are "productive" now—reading used to be for dreamers and other lazy pieces of shit, but now? Reading is *essential* to being an educated human being. And now, watching prestige television is basically the same thing. No wonder the latest Nicole Kidman limited series feels like work!

Is time *ever* truly free when you could be making money, improving yourself, or helping others? It's like an employer giving you "unlimited vacation" or Jesus saying "I'll forgive you but you have to feel super guilty about it all the time"[29]—it's a trap! And even if you do spend a fraction of it meaningfully engaging in a hobby or connecting with a friend, the rest might be spent swiping through your phone, worrying that you don't do anything interesting or that your friends are actually all hanging out without you. Sure, you could put your phone down and just *do* something, but who has the energy for that?

HOW TO RESIST MONETIZING YOUR HOBBY BY BEING BAD AT IT

Nurturing personal interests is vital to being a well-rounded person, and being a well-rounded person is a vital part of having a good "special skills" section on your resume. That's where hobbies come in: Whether it's collaging, baking, or *Real Housewives* reenacting (this is like Civil War reenacting except with epic *Real Housewives* fights), hobbies can help you unwind and remember to take enjoyment from things that aren't "productive" in a capitalistic sense. But when does a hobby cease to be leisurely and just become more work? The answer is when financial gain becomes involved! In the age of Etsy and people being obsessed with really lumpy ceramics, the threat of monetization has never loomed larger. Luckily, this hobby-to-labor pipeline can be avoided by producing things that no one in their right mind would want to pay you for.

---

28 Please note that this doesn't apply if you are currently en route to space with Pete Davidson. We hope he stays the course!

29 Jesus's sass and bitchiness has been lost in several translations of the Bible.

Here's how to resist turning that little thing you do just for you into another side hustle by simply being very bad at it:

Pick a hobby that is too hard for you.

If you've always wanted to learn an instrument and are considering picking up the ukulele or even guitar, stop right there and go for a cello. With enough practice, you could quickly master a simple instrument, and before you know it, you're getting ad revenue on your viral TikToks of ukulele Jack Harlow covers. No, thank you! Instead, pick up an impossibly large cello, an instrument at which it's way too late in the game for you to be even passably good at. Don't take lessons either; just grab that stick thing that you use to play it and go to town! You run no risk of monetizing your dreadful cover of "Whole Lotta Love" unless your neighbors offer to pay you to stop practicing.

Don't knit.

If you want to avoid turning your hobby into another soul-sucking money-making scheme, then avoid knitting at all costs. It doesn't matter how bad you are at it. In fact, the worse you are—the more weird holes and missed stitches and offensive bumps you create—the more likely it is that a skinny white girl with bleached eyebrows will try to buy the knit-monstrosity you created and wear it as a chic vest with a bike chain as a necklace. You'll be an adjunct professor as Parsons quicker than you can say, "I just wanted something I could do with my hands other than go on my phone while I watch TV."

Write incomprehensible erotic fanfiction.

If you want to do something that's just for you and do it poorly, then writing fanfiction is a great place to start. Pick any base text: *David Copperfield*, *Friends*, *Spider-Man: Turn Off the Dark*. What's important is that the content is highly sexual and the prose is offensively bad. You can really let your imagination run wild, and monetization is nearly impossible. You might even get a cease and desist! But then again, *Fifty Shades of Grey* was originally *Twilight* fanfic, so it's also possible that you'll get six book deals, then a $1.32 billion film franchise. God! Why can't anything just be a hobby?? Dakota Johnson doesn't have time to take on another project of this scale!

Explain memes to residents of a retirement home.

Perhaps the only hobby that runs no risk of monetization whatsoever, making unsolicited visits to seniors at your local retirement home and attempting to explain memes to them *will* be frustrating, but on the bright side, it will also *not* be lucrative. It's basically a guarantee that you'll be bad at this hobby because it is impossible, but it *will* give you an opportunity to spend time with an aging and vulnerable population. And if you're thinking, "Visiting the elderly feels more like an act of community service than a hobby," then you've got another think coming. Those single seniors are all fucking each other, and sitting through you trying to explain what a Chad is will only bring them vague concern for what the future of humanity is going to look like. This might just be the anti-capitalist hobby of your dreams! Just don't let anyone film it, because this content would absolutely go viral.

So use these approaches to keep your hobbies away from monetization's grasp! Grind culture found dead! Just like the seniors will pretend to be dead when you come to explain how memes evolved from "I Can Haz Cheezburger" to nihilistic poetry over an image of Paris Hilton.

Sigma Male? This Man Is Quietly Refusing to Orgasm Until He Can Afford a Tesla

He isn't wasting his time or his seed!

HOW I TOOK ON BIRDING TO RELAX, THEN STARTED MICROMANAGING THE BIRDS

By Ingrid Ostby

In my stressful 9-to-5, it was hard to find time for peace. Often, I would become so frustrated I would send messages to colleagues like, "I am confused as to why you did not notify me sooner of your urgent doctor's appointment" or "Please let me know as soon as you can why you didn't turn in your assignment when it was due two minutes ago."

I tried to be kind to them despite their poor performance. For example, I would let them out of work a full five minutes early, or bring in a tray of cookies, then stand next to the cookies the whole time to make sure no one took more than one (but also no less than one; allergies aren't an excuse to not be a team player!).

But still, my employees were testing my nerves so much with not being perfect that I needed a change—something to calm my nerves and lift my spirits. That's when I decided to take up a new hobby: birding.

What better way to de-stress than to spend time at home identifying birds by their calls, colors, and locations. I downloaded twenty birding apps so I could quickly become the best birder. I bought binoculars and Googled "most common birds near me." I even signed up for an online birding workshop but ultimately felt like the other students' questions were just slowing me down.

This was going to be my special time to focus on something other than work, and in turn grow as a person and chill out enough to deal with my employees, who are human and therefore make mistakes that are all, frankly, unforgivable—even though I love them like family and they're my best and only friends.

Over the next few weeks, I noticed the same birds coming in and out of my yard. It was so cute to notice their little patterns! For example, sometimes the robins would arrive a bit later than days prior, though the house sparrows were always prompt and present. Certain blue jays would do all the work of eating the peanuts I set out, which left none for the crows. Cardinals spent much of their time molting, which was productive for Q3, but overall—and I can't put my finger on it—I realized they're just not a good cultural fit for my backyard.

Clearly, the birds were not doing a good job at being birds, so I had to consider what type of performance plan I would put them on. First, I noted the two robins who were chronically late and began shooing them away in favor of other birds who actually made an effort to be on time according to a schedule

I made up and enforced simply to feel a sense of control in this fleeting mortal life.

Next, I took away some backyard benefits, like their beloved sunflower seeds. In my experience, you do not get good work out of employees—I mean birds—without starving them of positive reinforcement, like food to feed their bodies. Finally, I was starting to relax.

At this point, because I still felt upset that the birds were not being model birds, I just started doing their jobs for them. It was easier, because I am better at their jobs and have too many trust issues to delegate (I've tried to work through this in therapy, but I just don't trust shrinks).

I'd wake up at dawn, head out to the feeders, and eat all of their seed. I would bathe in the bird bath. I would climb into the trees and eat the peanuts I had set out for the blue jays and crows. By the time they arrived, they seemed confused to see me, their bird manager, eating and drinking the food I gave them but in a much more efficient and aesthetically pleasing way. The bluebird was especially confused, as I packed my smallest belongings and started moving into his birdhouse. If he wasn't going to bother flying around and being cute in a satisfactory manner, he didn't deserve to have a free place to "work on his nest."

I tried to tell them they could not take any time off from doing their bird work (hopping around and singing songs) while I was OOY (out of yard), because that would send a bad message to our superiors (Mother Nature, certain gods) who may visit the office and assume I don't run a tight ship and have failed to control the autonomous birds who have a life outside of my demands.

TIP:
Get a pair of binoculars! Then witness a heinous crime and start a new life in the witness protection program. Blank slate, baby!

Unfortunately things escalated when I noticed a grouping of interspecies birds in my yard. I could tell by their bird sounds that they were back-channelling, and I suspected they were either going to try to kill me or, worse, collectively bargain for equal rights to the food in my yard. I knew I had to shut this down, so I lit my yard on fire with gasoline and destroyed their natural habitat.

Try forming a cooperative in ruins, stupid birds.

In the end, I'm so glad I tried birding. It was such a great way to relax and really brought out the best of my managerial skills, even though my backyard is a fiery wasteland fit for neither bird nor human. I simply cannot wait to somehow use what I've learned as leverage against my employees. I think it'll be really relaxing for all of us.

ARE YOU DOING 'NOTHING' WRONG?

Our unrelenting work culture makes us feel like we must be "on" at all times, and this can leave us feeling exhausted and anxious. In order to remain healthy, we need to turn off once in a while and practice the beautiful art of doing nothing at all. Doing nothing is all about checking in on yourself and following your desires, so there's no one "right" way to do it. There are, however, many, many ways to do it wrong. Even a small mistake can render your nothing time completely unproductive (and not in the good way!). So if you're worried that you're doing "nothing" wrong, here's how to figure out why you're probably right (about being wrong):

When you're doing nothing, are you still thinking about work?

Look, we're not *shaming* you for not being able to disconnect from work—your boss is probably texting you about "Zoom happy hour" right now! You should really get back to them, because team bonding is really important. But if your brain can't enjoy the peaceful solitude of a cup of tea without thinking about work, then FUCK! Can you do anything right?! If you're struggling with finding a single moment of peace, you might need a full detox—move to a small coastal village for a few years and get in touch with nature so that you can finally find some meaning in being alive. Just don't stay too long, or you'll just be selfishly escaping from the real world and all its problems, don't you think? You could be earning money that could help people! But instead, you've chosen to do *nothing*? Do nothing better!

Are you "taking care of your body" or "buying into the self-care industrial complex"?

There is nothing more soothing than feeling warm water on your skin, getting in touch with your body, and disconnecting from the world for a brief moment in the day. But you absolutely *cannot* give in to the evil self-care industrial complex that tells you that you need to buy things to put in your bath to make yourself feel better. If you are soaking in a combination of essential oils, lotions, and weed suppositories to undo the forces of capitalism on your body, stop! Your "self-care" is just *perpetuating* capitalism! Thinking of using a bath bomb? STOP! You're just lining the pockets of Big Bath Bomb. You could try making your own soap, but that's just what The Man wants: having a busy, overworked woman performing extra labor on top of her soul-sucking day job. Why can't you just enjoy moisturizing your body with industrial-grade hospital lotion like a good person? Wait, you feel guilty now? You should stop that, too. Guilt is toxic!

Is your doing nothing intentionally anti-capitalist, or actually a reflection of your immense class privilege?

When you're doing your silly little idea of "nothing," are you actively fighting against the forces of capitalism that tell us we need to be consuming or producing something at all times? Or is it all because you have enough wealth and privilege to be able to "take some time off and reflect on things"? Wow, maybe you should have been volunteering this whole time?

Are you generating passive income while "doing nothing"?

Oh, now you're "earning income" while you're doing nothing? If you *are* doing that, like, can you tell us how? Theoretically speaking, how does one do that? Could you theoretically email us a detailed explanation? And none of that "sending over informative articles" bullshit, just tell us how to do it; you clearly have the time.

Remember: Doing nothing isn't a means to an end. It's a practice that acknowledges that your being and your time on this Earth require no justification. Doing nothing says, "I am whole." And if you find yourself in a gorgeous cabin upstate doing nothing and have the sudden urge to take photos of everything you're doing, then sorry, that's wrong, too. But like, could you send us pics, 'cause we kind of want to see them? Please?

Why I Made My Hobby My Job and My Job My Wife and My Wife My Hobby

I'm much happier now!

HOW TO RELAX IN THE BATH INSTEAD OF SPENDING THE WHOLE TIME WONDERING HOW LONG YOU'RE SUPPOSED TO STAY IN THERE

Baths have a long and rich history as a form of self-care. The earliest known bathhouses date back to 2500 BCE in the Indus Valley, or present-day Pakistan, and have social and spiritual significance across cultures as a way of restoring both the body and the mind. Now you can continue this relaxing tradition in your own life without even having to hit the local Turkish bathhouse! Having a soak at home is a wonderful way to unwind and reset, but what if as soon as you lower your tense little body into that tub, you can't think of anything else besides, "Here I am, just sitting in a bath," and "How long am I supposed to stay in here, exactly?" So you're bad at baths—big deal! We can't all be a depressed woman in a Wes Anderson movie. The good news is, all hope's not lost! Here's how you can properly enjoy this leisure activity instead of simply spending the whole time wondering if you're allowed to get out yet.

Don't bring your phone.
Bath time is the perfect opportunity to unplug, so leave that phone in the other room! You're supposed to be really present in this moment, and

attention-grabbing technology will only distract you with fun and entertainment. We'll be having none of that! Without your phone, not only will you have no distractions, you'll also have no sense of how much time has passed. The key here is to listen to your body, get in touch with your own desires, and use your intuition to know when you're ready to get out of the bath. Congratulations! You've been in the bath for three minutes.

Get high.

What could be chiller than smoking a doobie in the tub? You're basically the Big Lebowski (a self-care and relaxation king!). Getting a little buzz can help you attune your body to this sensory experience and let time slip away. Of course, smoking an entire joint in one sitting might also make you freak out. Like, where do I put it out? Also, there's no way this tub is clean enough for this to not be gross. What are those little bubbles around my skin? If your thoughts are going in a million directions, then you're probably too stressed to wonder what time it is or why the bath feels so cold all of a sudden. But if not, this might be awesome! This will probably kill another 2-4 minutes.

Read a book.

While mindless distractions are a no-go, reading a good book can heighten your enjoyment of this relaxing experience and help distract you from the nagging voice in your head that is constantly wondering how much time has passed. Pick a rich text and get ready for some deep and slow focus. Before you know it, you'll be saying, "Holy shit, there are twenty-seven pages left in this chapter and this bath is already lukewarm?" At least struggling to dry your fingertips before you turn the page will add a little time to the whole ordeal before you decide that you've had enough. Ah, the good life!

At the end of the day, no one is forcing you to take a bath, but you *do* have to do it. Look; we don't make the rules. Good luck!

Sick Fucks Who Sleep Nine Hours

Shelly Brice, 28

This sick fucking individual gets off on getting undressed and slithering into her little sleep dungeon around 10 p.m. every night (Why is she naked??). She usually sets her alarm for 6:45 a.m. and gets out of bed at 7 a.m., feeling "well-rested" and "ready to face the day." If that kind of sick shit is what it takes to "feel good," we'll pass!

Jesse Bontempo, 32

This nasty little freak says they "can't function" without nine full hours of having what we imagine are dirty little sex dreams. Jesse manages this most nights of the week by "putting their phone in another room before bedtime," probably because they're too busy thinking about horny dreams involving the entire cast of *The West Wing*—even Martin Sheen. Get help!!

Carissa Chen, 36

Look; we don't want to judge anybody's lifestyle choices, but this sick fuck will sleep anywhere from eight to eleven hours depending on what her body "needs" for that day (and apparently she has an insatiable need for being in bed, where sex happens?). Go listen to someone *else's* body, for once!

HERE'S WHAT YOU CAN DO TO SAVE THE WORLD

sponsored by an Oil Spill

With so much going on in the world today, we can sometimes feel powerless in the face of larger forces that are destroying our beautiful planet. But no matter how uncertain our future can be, remember that change always and very specifically starts with YOU. So if you're wondering what you can do in your free time to make a difference, ignore the oil spill that just dumped millions of gallons of oil into the Gulf coast (everybody makes mistakes!), and focus on these five things *you* can do to solve climate change and *literally change the world.*

Carry your groceries in a reusable canvas tote.

Instead of using wasteful plastic bags that almost inevitably end up in the ocean, threatening wildlife and humans alike (who would do that?), pick up some reusable tote bags for grocery shopping instead! You'll feel great when you put your plastic forks and plastic trash bags in your canvas NPR tote. That's *one* less piece of plastic to get caught in this oil slick. Power to the people!

Save water by combining all the showers you take into one big shower.

Sure, you gave up baths years ago, but did you know your personal use of water is wasting thousands of gallons of our most precious natural resource every second? Try taking fewer showers, or just combining all your showers into one big shower, and you can get us one step closer to a more sustainable planet. When you think about it, it's actually so empowering that you can save the world with your little sacrifices. We (the oil spill now spreading over hundreds of nautical miles) are counting on you!!

When ordering takeout, ask them to put the food directly in your hands.

We all know that takeout and delivery contributes to unnecessary waste that isn't always recycled, so next time you order pad thai to-go, ask them to just put it directly in your hands. It's a little awkward at first, but everyone will appreciate your commitment to living sustainably, and you might inspire other people to do something this wildly impractical, which will make you feel amazing! Whatever you do, don't Google "oil spill Gulf duck sad." Bad for the environment!!

Painstakingly replace every plastic straw with a metal straw.

Plastic straws are the most wasteful, unnecessary contribution to plastic waste, and one way you can let everyone know that is by swapping out every straw you see with a brand-new, reusable metal straw. Of course, all these straws will come with plastic and cardboard packaging, and have to be flown across the country using fossil fuels, too, but it's all for the greater good, right guys? Aw, it's kind of like we're saving the planet together!

Beat yourself with your own garbage while repeating *"mea culpa"* until it fully degrades into biomass.

Take all of your non-recyclable trash, put it in a satchel, and throw it over your back, over and over while you repent for your earthly sins, which could last upwards of 1000 years. Compost takes a long time to break down, so pace yourself! If everyone did this, imagine the destruction we could wreak while you're busy feeling guilty!

We all have something to contribute to end climate change and change the world. Just remember, you have to believe that every little bit counts. Or else, what is all this for? Now get out there and buy some LED light bulbs!

Congratulations! You Are Reading a Book

You did it. You've come very close to finishing a book. How does it feel? Good, we bet. The rest is just an easy downhill coast. All you have to do is keep turning some pages before you can feel the sweet release of being done with a book. Soon, all your pain will be gone, and you'll finally be free again. Enjoy the ride!

HOW TO MEDITATE EVEN THOUGH THAT'S WHEN YOU ALWAYS THINK OF YOUR BEST TWEETS

It can be so hard to come up with good ideas in a society that pressures us to always be making content—there are so many distractions that it can be nearly impossible to ever sit and think of something new. And while many wise people throughout history have turned to meditation in order to find peace and clarity, those people did not have a personal brand to uphold on various social media platforms or the constant, nagging fear that if you don't post something, you will cease to exist. If you've been one of the many people trying to get into meditation to clear your mind and be more focused, but all that happens is that you think of your sickest tweets, here's how to push through it and keep going in spite of the fact that the tweet is very, very good and you have to write it down before you forget.

Remember to forgive yourself for having such incredible thoughts at the wrong time.

If you have a fleeting thought while meditating, let it go. Nobody is perfect! Although technically, that thought you had might have actually been perfect? Letting it go feels like such a waste of an idea. Like, why even meditate to be better at thinking if you're gonna just let such impossibly good thoughts go like that? But no, now is the time for meditating, not brilliance. Focus up and stop thinking!

Ask yourself: Is it really a good tweet or just good in the way that your late-night Notes app thoughts are "good"?

Without getting too off-task, ask yourself: Does this thought actually have legs, or am I just so excited at the thought of having a fully formed thought come to me in such a natural way that I'm using it as an excuse to stop meditating? Say it out loud. Is it something like, "Why does it feel weird to eat peanut butter off of a knife even though it's easier to clean than a spoon"? Okay, that's pretty compelling. Maybe you should just tweet it then get right back to meditating. You won't be distracted by the burning desire to check if anyone's liked it, probably.

Focus on your breath.

When the thoughts start flowing, remember to focus on your breath. And if you start to feel like you're forgetting brilliant ideas, like "meditation is really like an escape room but from your thoughts," just remember that you really don't need to tweet that. Instead, ask yourself: Why is it that all your thoughts come in the form of tweets?

Just make it your mantra!

Still can't stop thinking about how "grapes are the sausages of fruit"? Go ahead and make that your mantra for this session. You'll say it over and over until it loses all meaning to you whatsoever, and ideally when you are done meditating, you will realize that it still has no meaning.

Learning how to breathe through a fucking brilliant idea and letting it go can be hard, but meditation is all about learning to breathe through the suffering. Hopefully you can work through it and let that idea about gay dogs slide this time. But if not, we totally get it—your 304 followers are gonna love this!

Wow! This Woman Is In an Emotionally Abusive, Psychosexual Relationship with the Duolingo Owl

WOMAN DECIDES TO COUNT APPENDECTOMY AS VACATION

By *Mara Wilson*

After not having more than two consecutive days off in several years, twenty-nine-year-old hostess and bartender Stefanie Lima has decided to go ahead and count the emergency removal of her appendix and subsequent healing process as a nice vacation away from it all.

"Just the day before, I was telling my girlfriend that I felt so run-down and tired, and I could really use a break," says Lima. "Then the next day, I woke up covered in sweat, feeling like someone was stabbing me in the stomach, and thought, 'I guess this is my chance!'"

Lima's trip started in style, being luxuriously carried out of her apartment by two paramedics.

"She decided we would splurge and surprised me with an ambulance!" Lima says of her girlfriend, Dani Mitchell. "I told her we could just drive, but she insisted I go all out, I guess because this is my first real vacation in my adult life."

"Also, I was in so much pain that she couldn't move me out of our bed, and I threw up all over her when she tried," adds Lima. "But now I just think of it as a funny thing that happened while I was on vacation."

After a scenic drive through downtown San Diego in a windowless ambulance, Lima was treated to all kinds of cool new sights at the hospital.

"I'd never gotten a CT scan before!" she says. "And for a second, before the anesthesia kicked in, I got to see what a real OR looks like! It's just like on *Grey's*."

Following a successful laparoscopic appendectomy, Lima kicked back with a nice cocktail of Dilaudid, Pregablin, Zofran, and saline, and spent the night in a hospital bed while Mitchell slept in a chair.

"I told Dani that she could climb into my hospital bed, but the nurses said no," says Lima. "Still, it was kind of nice not to have to make our bed or worry about what to have for breakfast. We still haven't made any vacation friends, but there's time. I was hoping for one of the nurses, but probably not after the whole bed thing."

As soon as she was able to hold her phone upright by herself, Lima was sure to make the most of her stay with lots of Instagram stories of her IV, her bandages, and her feet in hospital socks, with captions like, "The world is a book, those who stay home read only one page."

"I told her to text me as soon as she felt well enough, but the first thing she sent me was an out-the-window photo of a palm tree in the hospital parking lot," says Lima's cousin, Tina Ramos. "She even sent me a little palm tree emoji with it."

"Maybe she forgot there's like thousands of palm trees here," suggests Ramos, who also lives in San Diego.

Back at home, Lima continued her slowed-down pace, where she enjoyed "a ton" of tropical-flavored Jell-O and took lots of long, romantic walks with Mitchell down the hallway of their apartment building to release gas and prevent blood clots.

"We also watched *The Gilded Age*," says Lima, though she now has no memory of it. "It was about trains, I think?"

"Stef kept talking about the matching tattoos we got when we went to Mexico for her twenty-first birthday," says Mitchell. "Then she'd point to her scars and say, 'I've got something to remember *this* by, too!'"

Overall, Lima's little trip cost her $14,467. She admits that she was shocked at the price and will have to set up a GoFundMe to cover the costs, but remembers that it's "only about $10,000 more" than a trip to Cabo.

"And yeah, I am still coming down off a lot of drugs, and I have these gas pains that feel like tiny electric shocks inside my body," says Lima, "but it was ten days without work!

"It would have been two weeks," she adds, "but they called and asked if I could come in, because Connor, who usually covers for me, is doing the vacation thing, too, after a loose shelf of liquor fell and hit him on the head."

"At least we can trade vacay pics when he's back!"

Spa Day? This Woman Had Several Precancerous Moles Removed

HOW TO JUST KIND OF SIT THERE ON THE PLANE

So your plane is stuck on the tarmac for an hour—not good! But oh no, your phone battery is at 1 percent, the Wi-Fi is inexplicably down, and there are no screens on this discount flight. Is this legal? Will you die? Here's how to make the best of just kind of . . . you know, sitting there?

Control your fight-or-flight response.

In spite of the feelings arising that this is the moment that will ultimately kill you, remember that this is not a dangerous situation. The plane is on the ground. Just because you are alone with your own thoughts doesn't mean you are in actual danger!

Talk to someone!

The person sitting next to you is probably just as scared as you are. Try to find common ground and a sense of courage in the face of fear. Oh, their phone is alive? And they have headphones in and are watching a true crime documentary they downloaded? Maybe you can lean over and try to read the lips of—nope, they're onto you and pivoted away. Alone again.

Try some new ways to sit.

Shake up your routine and see what it's like to sit up straight, or with a leg crossed—anything but the fetal position you've curled into. It's not helping!

Pretend you're a guard at Buckingham Palace if they were sitting on a plane.

Make sitting like a statue a fun, ironic activity you choose to do! Just try to avoid thinking about how much it sucks you can't record this.

Start yelling your political manifesto until you're arrested and removed from the plane.

You wouldn't be the first to do this to get out of an unexplained delay!

Sitting anywhere can be a frustrating and overwhelming experience. Just remember that you're okay and it will be over soon. Unless there is a gate change—then sorry, someone is probably going to die!

The Attention Economy, Explained

In this day and age, our attention is our most valuable resource, and countless businesses are longing to capture it. If you were wondering how the attention economy is robbing you of your autonomy, your time, and your wellbeing, we're going to break down exactly what to do to

You have reached your free articles for the month.
Please subscribe to continue reading.

I QUIT MY JOB TO MAKE CONTENT AND TRAVEL THE WORLD. HERE'S WHY I'D NOW RATHER HAVE A JOB WITH HEALTHCARE BENEFITS AND A 401K

By Madison Dillard

When I was working at my 9-to-5 job as an accountant, I always dreamed of one day packing up all my stuff and traveling around the world. The only problem was that I didn't know how to make an income off of it. Luckily, after the popularity of TikTok started to rise, I saw hundreds of accounts making a living from traveling the world, making content about it, then earning money from sponsored opportunities and brand partnerships. After doing my research, I decided that I could live that life, too. I just didn't realize that it actually wouldn't be that great and I'd desperately wish I had my old job back because it had an actual salary and benefits.

I saved up my money for years, researched the places I wanted to go, and made all of the travel plans necessary to finally accomplish my dream of being a citizen of the world. Once I finally put in my two weeks at my accounting job, I decided that the first thing I was going to do was travel around Mexico, starting with Mexico City. When I first got there, I decided to let the city take me anywhere it wanted me to go. It turns out that the city initially wanted me to have forty-eight hours of traveler's diarrhea, which is actually pretty hard to make aspirational content out of. But there aren't any sick days in the world of monetized wanderlust!

I thought that using lots of hashtags and taking pictures of the beach, beautiful architecture, and myself in a bikini would get the attention of millions, but sadly, I found myself begging other travel influencers on TikTok and Instagram for a "promo for promo," which was somehow more demoralizing than eating a microwave Amy's Mac n' Cheese in my cubicle.

After three long months of traveling around Mexico, I got my first brand partnership, and I was beyond thrilled. When I got the DM from a popular clothing store, I thought to myself, "Yes! I've finally made it!" They told me they wanted me to do a really specific shoot where I needed at least five people wearing different outfits entirely made up of their clothes and accessories. I thought, "Wow, that's it? How much does it pay?" and then they told me it pays in . . . clothes. I guess selling your soul for clout and contributing to a retirement fund are both equally valid ways of investing in yourself! Right?

Is it normal for your hair to fall out while you're traveling or is that more of a stress thing?

Anyway, they did *repost* my content though, which gave me a little exposure, just without any money whatsoever, which is another part of my old job that I really miss.

After that opportunity, I got a lot more DMs asking to sponsor my travels through Central America, and I felt like I could actually feed myself for a few weeks. It was everything that I dreamed about while I was staring out the window during all-staff meetings, imagining a more spontaneous, adventurous life that I saw on Instagram. However, after being forced to treat a yeast infection "homeopathically" while living in a van in a suburban parking lot, I realized that, yeah, I actually would like that health insurance back. Even the bad kind with the high deductible.

The last straw came five months later when I shattered my ankle while hiking a mountain trail for an athleisure brand in Aspen. The injury required surgery and I was in the hospital for three days afterwards, which left me thinking, "Would going back to my accountant job really be such a bad thing?"

Suddenly the idea of two weeks' vacation sounded infinitely better than falling off a small cliff, then falling off an even bigger cliff, only to be mistaken for a wounded deer and shot at by local hunters.

Sure, I'd probably be depressed and feel creatively limited, but I'd also have my old insurance and a 401k again, without the threat of losing all my money or possibly dying. Life is really all about choices.

So after two years of traveling around the world (or really just Central and North America), I've decided to pack it up again and go back to my salaried job as an accountant in Charlotte, North Carolina. I might be deeply unhappy working at a job that I've always hated, but at least I'll be able to afford the therapy sessions I'll use to talk about it!

TIP:

Take a "camping trip" vacation in your backyard. If you don't have a backyard, set up a tent in your living room. If your living room isn't big enough to set up a tent, just take a shower!

HOW TO STRUCTURE YOUR FREE TIME WHEN YOU'RE CONSTANTLY BEING HUNTED

By Seth Rubin

Free time can be hard to come by, so you want to be sure that you're making the most of yours when you have it. These days, with the lines between work and play becoming increasingly blurred, it can be challenging to set aside time for rest and relaxation—even more so when you're constantly being hunted by a mysterious, unseen enemy. If you're concerned about making the most of your free time but also need to sleep with one eye open, read on to learn our top ten tips for structuring your precious free time when you're also dealing with the unique burden of being relentlessly hunted for sport.

Create a schedule.

Creating—and sticking to—a schedule can be invaluable for making the most of your free time. By clearly defining when you're working, when you're relaxing, and when you're moving from bunker to bunker wearing your all-black hiding clothes, you can easily structure your free time. Pro tip: don't forget to carve out a few minutes every day to free-scream, "Why are they hunting me? Oh God, why are they hunting me?!" But scream into a pillow or in sign language so they can't hear you. #ProductivityGoals!

Get a hobby.

Take a note from the many people who are constantly hunting you and get your very own hobby! A hobby can be a fun, productive way to spend your free time, and there are options for everyone: Try joining a pick-up basketball league (that plays somewhere with lots of places to take cover, like the woods), working on your forgery skills (to design the fake passport of your dreams), or even wine tasting!

TIP:
Freaky Friday with a bear so you can fuck other bears—I mean, so you can finally hibernate.

Burnt out on arts and crafts? Channel your frustration at being hunted into a killer stand-up comedy routine, with jokes like, "Hey, what's the deal with being hunted when you're just trying to attend your niece's baptism?" You know what they say: Laughter, along with a supply of homemade tourniquets and a reliable unmarked van, is the best medicine!

Be flexible.

When it comes to being an adult, you simply can't do it all! Try combining hobbies, like crafting while also listening to a podcast, or throat-punching the guy attacking you with nunchucks while also listening to a podcast. Flexibility is more than the key to the perfect roundhouse kick—it's also crucial for achieving perfectly balanced free time. Just don't forget to finish the job, or he will return!

Learn mindfulness.

Mindfulness is all about being present in the moment and making choices with intention. Try embracing mindfulness by impulsively saying "yes" to coffee with an old friend, or using them as a human shield when that one guy with knives for hands tries to stab you in a Starbucks! You'll return to work feeling refreshed, fulfilled, and still alive (for now).

Get comfortable saying "no."

We're conditioned to say yes to everything, but sometimes a simple "no" can do wonders for your self-care by allowing you to free up some more time for yourself. For example: "I'm sorry, I'm just too busy today to meet for drinks." "No thank you! I would not like to be hunted today, not on the day of my niece's baptism!" and "No. I refuse to die. Take me to the Yakuza boss who placed the bounty on my head or I will burn down your racetrack" are all simple phrases that will help you get used to saying "no" and having more time to focus on *you.*

Balance long-term and short-term goals.

Are you struggling to achieve your short- and long-term goals? Write a list for yourself! Some common short-term goals include "doing yoga twice a week" and "learning assassin's German," while long-term goals can range from "learning how to clean a gun while blindfolded" to "destroying the nest of vampire hitmen who sleep under the docks during the day and hunt you at night." You're gonna have great stories to tell when your coworkers ask what you were up to over the weekend.

Make wellness part of your day.

Work is great, but it's not everything: Your health comes first! Fill your free time with wellness activities, such as running (perfect for helping you avoid hired goons in crowded city streets) or even rock climbing (to help you escape the guy with knives for hands when he pops out of a fruit pyramid at your favorite two-story Whole Foods). And don't forget about foot peels! Who doesn't love a foot peel? Just be wary of the man who is hiding in your bathtub.

TIP:
You don't owe anyone an elaborate blood sacrifice. Even on the solstice!

Get an accountability buddy.

There's nothing like an "accountabilibuddy" to help ask you the tough questions, like, "Did you achieve your goals today?" or "Where have you been for the last seventeen months?" or "What is that red dot on your forehead?" Just be sure to vet them ahead of time, or you'll end up having to tearfully execute another acquaintance in the pouring rain. Not fun for anyone!

Monetize your hobbies.

Why do something fun for free when you can do something fun and get paid for it? For example, if you make your own jewelry, consider opening an Etsy shop—okay, we're pretty sure they've stopped reading. Look, you're in danger. That's right, they found you again—no, we don't know how, either. Just grab that bug-out bag from under your bed, and we'll meet you at the safe house. Put down those resin earrings! Go! Go now!

Eat well.

Whether or not you're being hunted by a rogue's gallery of cold-blooded killers (like right now), a fiber-rich diet packed with vitamins and nutrients will help keep you regular throughout your day! This might be your last chance to eat for days, so use your time wisely, but then again, it might already be too late. #ProductivityGoals!

So there you have it: the top ten tips for structuring your free time while you're constantly being hunted by a mysterious squad of elite assassins. Don't forget to set aside time each week to clean the chemical toilets in your vast network of underground bunkers. You got this!

WHY I'M SAVING MOTHERHOOD FOR RETIREMENT

Ever since I was a little girl, I've always wanted to be a mother. I always dreamed of the day that I would get to raise a beautiful, special human being and give it all the love it deserves. But now that I'm an adult with a demanding job and $50,000 in college debt, I've realized that some dreams just need to be deferred—like travel, fancy dinners out, and the decades-long process of raising my own progeny. That's why I've decided to save motherhood for the season of my life where I'll finally have both the time and money for a baby: retirement!

This decision was a hard one, since so many of my friends are having kids in their twenties and their thirties, but all I see is a generation of overworked, depressed people squandering the best years of their lives changing diapers and paying for daycare while barely scraping by. Why not save it for when you don't have all those burdens? Like between the age of seventy-two and seventy-five, specifically?

Some of my friends say things like, "More people are having children in their forties, which you can still do," and "You know you won't be fertile in your seventies, right? Right, Shannon? You do know this?" and I'm like, okay, fair—but by the time I'm forty, I will finally be in my prime earning years, and raising a baby in that time would completely get in the way of my goal of raising a baby.

As for the other point—please. I'll probably be more fertile when I'm not under all this stress from work.

I took a few long, hard years wondering how I would manage a child with a two-week maternity leave and $30k a year in day care costs. For all that money, I wouldn't even get to see my own baby grow into a tiny human? That seems like a pretty shitty deal. That's when I realized I'll be able to give my baby the attention it deserves when I'm just kind of old and catching up on the entire *Housewives* franchise while hurtling ever closer to my own death.

Why spend thousands of dollars on day care when you could simply save parenting for the end of your life? Plus, by the time I raise them into a fully grown person, I'll be nearing ninety and ready for a strapping young person to take care of me. The timing simply couldn't make more sense.

Sure, I do wish that I lived in a country that valued motherhood and family enough to support babies and give everyone healthcare. Did you know IVF is free in France? All of these things sure sound great. But as long as I'm here in the United States, putting off this grueling, gratifying experience feels right for me and my baby. And when my skin is more dry and paperlike, my bone density is decreased and I finally begin to shrink, I'll be ready to have my baby. Yes, one baby, because those things are fucking EX-PEN-SIVE.

Now, all I have to do is save millions of dollars and hope that the stock market doesn't crash, because lord knows Social Security won't be a thing in 2060.

Here's to family planning!

Missed Opportunity? In the Amount of Time This Woman Has Spent Rewatching a Sitcom She Enjoyed, She Could Have Read *Anna Karenina* in Russian, Which She Would Have Hated

"EVERYONE FROM COLLEGE IS REPULSED BY YOUR LACK OF CREATIVE OUTPUT" AND OTHER THINGS YOUR IDIOT THERAPIST DOESN'T UNDERSTAND

by Sio Hornbuckle

Therapy can work wonders for the common man. Unfortunately, what they often don't realize is that your problems are much bigger and more important than anything they could possibly comprehend. So, while your therapist's advice might work for herself and her other, less deep and complex clients, not a single one of whom has ever made *Forbes*' "30 Under 30," it can sometimes fall flat for a thought leader like you. We compiled some high-achieving career complaints your fucking idiot therapist just doesn't understand.

"Everyone from college is repulsed by your lack of creative output."

Remember that one person from your Introduction to French class? They're on *Grey's Anatomy* now. It was just a single episode and their dad is on Shonda Rhimes' racquetball team, but still. When they posted behind-the-scenes photos on Instagram, all your school friends commented to congratulate them. Then they probably scrolled down and saw the photo you posted of your unfamous aunt blowing out her birthday candles and fell violently ill. It keeps them up at night, the way you've wasted your one precious life. If your therapist says you're projecting, she's just trying to protect your feelings. She has no idea what it's like to fall so far behind. Her friends are all just doctors.

"You tried meditation once. It literally does not work on your brain, and it will never work."

It is physically and spiritually impossible for you to ever benefit from meditation. You know this. She'll say to keep trying, but she doesn't get how precious your time is. Sitting in silence for thirty minutes, multiple times a week? You could be rewatching Aaron Sorkin's *Masterclass*.

"If your parents had bought you ice skates when you asked for them in first grade, you would be a retired Olympian by now and you wouldn't have any problems."

You have naturally good balance, but it's too late to cash in. Your therapist has never seen you at a roller rink, so she'll probably tell you not to dwell on hypotheticals. But God, you could have been a star, and you should resent your mom and dad forever.

"Your nose is kind of weird and that's why no one will ever listen to your ideas."

Your therapist will either tell you that your nose is normal or that you're overestimating other people's awareness of your weird nose. She's coddling you and it's wrong of her. Other people notice your weird nose. It's right there in the center of your face. It's all they can think about when you're trying to explain why you deserve success beyond their wildest imaginations, and it's at least half the reason why they will never give it to you. It's not an insecurity—it's objective truth!

"There's more pressure on you than previous generations because you have to EGOT before climate change fallout makes it pointless and maybe even kind of embarrassing to EGOT."

How would your therapist understand? She got her doctorate way before her achievements could be overshadowed by climate catastrophe. You're not so lucky. On top of EGOTing, you have to hope that people still care about EGOTing by the time you do it. It's totally possible that you'll EGOT and everyone will be like, *It's bad to be a creative now. What are you doing? This is how you're spending your time? Do you know what's going on in the world?*

"You're getting older at a faster rate than everyone else."

She'll try to reason with you using logic, but she's off base. It's obvious just by looking into your eyes that you were cursed by an angry witch and now you're doomed to wither away to a husk within years, if not minutes. Your friends can take their sweet time exploring career options, but it's all a little more urgent for you.

"No one takes you seriously as an artist because of that time you said 'acai' wrong at a party three years ago."

Everyone heard. They told their friends and family, and their friends and family told *their* friends and family, and now everyone knows. Your therapist will say everyone mispronounces things sometimes, but she's wrong. These people don't, and they can't believe you would speak with such unearned confidence. They'll never trust the authority of your voice again.

TIP:
Feeling lazy? Binge-watch TV in a way that somehow still feels like work.

"If you stop working for one single day, God will see that you are ungrateful for the gift of life. He will send down a plague of locusts. You will bring about the end of times."

This is objectively true. Your therapist just doesn't get the grind.

HOW TO RELIEVE YOUR GUILT FOR HAVING TO PARTICIPATE IN SOCIETY, THEN DEAL WITH THE GUILT YOU HAVE FOR FEELING THAT RELIEF

It happens to everyone: You feel guilty for simply having to participate in our broken society and economic system. Then, you realize that your guilt isn't serving anyone and feel some sense of relief, right before a fresh wave of guilt comes crashing on the shores of your consciousness as you feel terrible and undeserving of your acceptance of feeling okay for a second. Such is the cycle of life! But it doesn't have to be this way. Here's how to manage this complicated cycle of emotions:

Take action.
You shouldn't feel guilty for just doing the things you need to get by, but if you're really troubled by the injustices of the world around you, then make part of your life fighting for a better future! The major issue with this option is that it is hard.

Go to therapy.
When you are in therapy, that is *your* time. You can say anything, feel anything, and it's all good! You paid for your forty-five minutes, and you're not taking anything away from anyone. But then again, couldn't that time and money be better spent elsewhere? Is complaining to a quiet, highly educated person really the answer? Oh, the guilt. THE GUILT, MAMA.

Go full nihilist.
If you haven't found any way to live that adheres to your moral compass, throw out the compass altogether! Just say, "Nothing matters or means anything," and then immediately begin to analyze how your ability to take on that attitude comes from a place of relative privilege. Then feel guilty for feeling guilty instead of doing something about anything. Shit!

Become a Republican.
If the constant, nagging feeling of guilt and accountability is too much, go Republican and you will literally never experience "guilt" again! This might seem cool at first, but you're gonna have to do a lot of work to convince

yourself capitalism is a meritocracy, and then if things aren't going well for you, you're going to feel a lot of anger.

Become a Democrat.

Blame everything on Republicans. This will be hard if you have any inclination to look inward.

Become a Disney Adult.

This is the only one that actually works. Is it worth it? That's up to you.

RELAXING! THIS WOMAN LIT A $38 CANDLE AND IS THINKING ABOUT HOW MUCH EVERY HOUR OF BURN TIME COSTS

In the everyday hustle and bustle of modern life, it's vital to carve out time for relaxation and decompression. Between her job, grad school coursework, and general efforts to stay alive, twenty-eight-year-old Maddie Beckett is doing just that by lighting a fancy scented candle and then deeply stressing about how much every hour of burn time actually costs.

"I bought this $38 rosemary and sea salt candle last year, but I never burn it because I don't know what warrants use of such a costly little scented fire," Maddie says. "But today I was feeling so overwhelmed and stressed out, I just decided to pour myself a glass of wine, kick my feet up, and splurge on the candle I already bought but feel guilty about burning."

However, Maddie's stress has only heightened during this period of would-be unwinding, as she's spent every moment calculating the cost of the candle's burn time.

"This candle is eight ounces and will allegedly burn for forty hours, making every hour of burn time cost ninety-five cents," she says. "So if I burn this for three hours, that's $2.85, which is more than one subway fare, or approximately 1.7 honeycrisp apples."

While Maddie originally intended to write in her gratitude journal and do some light stretching during her candle time, she instead wound up running a cost-benefit analysis of using the candle which she did purchase specifically to burn.

"I just ran to take the trash out, but then my sister called me and so I chatted with her for a bit outside," Maddie says. "That whole time the candle was burning for nothing and no one in my apartment. That's ten minutes down the drain."

Maddie is currently on the fence about whether she should blow the candle out but is using its invigorating fragrance to help power her game plan.

"Maybe I should get pregnant so that my sense of smell will become more sensitive and I'll get more bang for my buck on this thing," she says. "But then of course there's also the risk that I'll find the scent nauseating, especially during the first trimester, and there goes, like, twenty-eight bucks."

"*But*," Maddie adds, "if I find it nauseating, then I won't burn it at all, and that will save me a lot of money. Like, almost enough to offset the cost of raising a child."

This line of thought led Maddie down considering the ethics of conceiving a biological child during the late stages of impending climate crisis, personal questions about her maternal instinct, reflections on her fear of commitment and the daunting prospect of coparenting, then ultimately Googling how expensive it is to freeze your eggs.

"Fuck," Maddie says. "I'm more stressed out now than when I started. I'm gonna have to burn this candle for at least another two hours just to unwind from everything I just learned about egg freezing. There goes another 190 cents, adjusted for inflation!"

THREE GIRLS' NIGHT DENTAL PROCEDURES TO PERFORM ON EACH OTHER 'CAUSE YOUR INSURANCE DOESN'T COVER IT

Sometimes there's nothing more rejuvenating than a good old fashioned girls' night in. Who needs a crowded bar with expensive, sugary cocktails—especially when those sugary cocktails hurt your weak enamel, and you don't have dental insurance? Whether you cook a meal together, watch a good movie, or just de-stress and talk about life, spending quality time with your girls, gays, and theys can be healing and restorative. That's why we suggest you skip the club this weekend, put on your PJs, and just stay in performing these essential dental procedures on each other because your insurance doesn't cover it. Girls' night!

Cavity filling!

Just like a glass of cold pinot gris, you can't go wrong with this classic dental procedure! Even those with the finest oral health can end up with the occasional cavity, and if one of your girls is left untreated, they can lead to significant tooth decay. We're not in the business of explaining *how* to fill a cavity at home, mostly because we don't want to get sued, but we definitely suggest you go for it, babe! You may not be able to get your hands on any novocaine, so maybe hit up your sketchiest cousin and see if they know anyone who sells percs. Again, this is *not* medical advice, hun. With your body loose on opioids (the "dentist" and "patient" should both pop a couple to stay on the same page and because it's fun) and the drill from when your artsy friend briefly decided they were gonna get into tattooing on full blast, you'll be doing whatever it is a dentist does to a cavity in no time. This is the sort of bonding you could never achieve if your insurance covered dental!

Root canal!

Not for the faint of heart, a root canal involves deep drilling to remove infected pulp from the root of the tooth. Yuck! You shouldn't perform or undertake an unlicensed root canal unless the need for one has been prescribed by a real endodontist, but on girls' night, we all like to break the rules a little. Maybe once your endodontist states you need a root canal and tells you the out-of-pocket cost, you can casually mention that you're going to have your friend do it over tacos with a makeshift drill (vibrator and a Bobby pin sterilized by

Tonya's lighter). She might feel some moral responsibility to do the procedure at a reduced rate, but she might not! In fact, you might be better off trying to get her to join your friend group. Then there could be girls' night root canals for everyone!

Gum grafting!

A gum graft is a surgical procedure generally performed by a periodontist with the use of anesthesia and involves grafting tissue from the roof of your mouth onto your receding gums. Having your graphic designer friend give you a gum graft can save you from such issues as major medical debt and a super boring trip to the dentist. Grab a glass of wine and relish in the fact that the medicinal and the social have always been interwoven. Did you know that in the 1700s, ether was a party drug until some guy broke his leg while at an "ether frolic" and didn't feel any pain, so then dentists were like, "Whoa, we should use this on our patients." This is sort of like the opposite of that. Hope this helps!

So cut loose with your besties by performing these dental procedures that your insurance won't cover on each other. Once you get comfortable with this, you might even graduate to administering other procedures, like an appendectomy or Lasik. This is mutual aid at its finest!

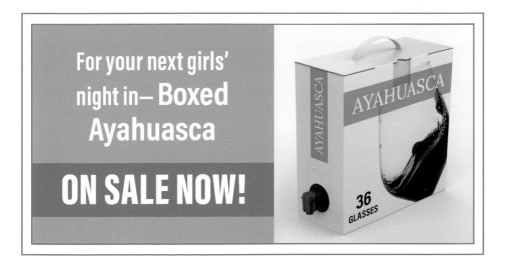

WHY DO YOU WANT TO SAVE BABY TURTLES?
EVERYONE THINKS THEY'RE CUTER THAN YOU

by ExxonMobil

Here at ExxonMobil, we are dedicated to being a green company, which, to us, means being generally good and nice! That's why we take everyone's concerns seriously, including yours about the "endangerment" of baby sea turtles due to polution (sp?). However, we can't help but wonder, like, why do you *want* to save them? Everyone thinks they're so much cuter than you and everybody's talking about it.

Extracting the Earth's natural resources allows you to lead the comfortable little life you enjoy with your streaming services and your fifteen-minute grocery delivery, and we're happy to provide you with that. But that wasn't enough for you, was it? You had to watch a video of some baby sea turtles dying of natural causes probably and get all mad about it. And that's so valid. We actually love baby turtles, too! They're so cute, oh my God. With their tiny little heads and their sweet little baby eyes. Most people would say that by comparison, you look like an absolute giant monster freak—and they are saying that! A lot! It's basically the first thing people mention when you come up.

Of course, that sort of thing doesn't really get to you because you're so selfless. You know that everyone absolutely loves baby turtles and donates money to help them all the time, even though your mom is the only one who really loves you unconditionally and you still go to parties where people who call themselves your "friends" ask you to Venmo them $5 for lukewarm beer. I bet they'd never do that to a baby turtle. They would probably pay $5 to watch a baby turtle drink a beer. It just seems so unfair. But you don't care about that sort of thing, we guess. We would be so pissed!! It's amazing you let people treat you so badly. ☺

Remember when being green was something that we all did together? We all stood hand-in-hand, ExxonMobil executives and middle schoolers all at the same level of effort, and did things like take shorter showers and recycle, kind of? Everyone was having fun. But then everyone decided to hate "corporations" (which are people, and hating people is antisemitism sometimes depending on the people, so maybe think about that). Now all anyone wants to do is "hold politicians accountable for being in Big Oil's pocket" and talk about how you "don't look like Harvey Weinstein, but between a baby turtle and Harvey Weinstein, you're definitely closer to Harvey than to the turtle."

We just think it's wrong.

So get out there and fight the good fight, whatever that means to you! Here at Exxon, we believe in individual freedom and the ability for individuals to make a change. Just be careful if that good fight involves showing your boyfriend pictures of baby sea turtles, because he'll almost definitely realize how grotesque you are in comparison and leave you!

Woman Hoped She Would Have Been Raptured by Now

WOW! THIS WOMAN'S RETIREMENT PLAN IS THE SIXTH EXTINCTION

Every generation retires differently, and it's easy to forget that the idea of "retirement" is still a relatively new concept. While Baby Boomers have faced a relative lack of retirement security compared to the Silent Generation before them, for younger workers with less traditional career paths today, retirement feels like a logistical impossibility. Social security? Roth IRA? What does it all mean? Well, one woman is taking an approach that throws the need to understand these concepts out the window.

Meet Eden Wilson: a free-thinking twenty-six-year-old whose retirement plan is the Sixth Extinction, the final extinction happening as a result of human intervention in the natural processes of the planet.

While some of Eden's peers scramble, worrying about savings or family planning, Eden is simply waiting for the Anthropocene extinction to come to a close, ending all human life on Earth.

"The last mass extinction happened 65 million years ago," says Eden. "So, we're really due for one, plus or minus a few years. The climate crisis should hopefully speed that up a bit."

"Just imagine if the avian dinosaurs who got taken out by the Cretaceous mass extinction had been stressing out about retirement or 'planning' for the 'future,'" Eden adds. "What an epic waste of time that'd be! They'd all feel so foolish. That's why I'm not risking the same mistake by planning for financial security in my most vulnerable life stages."

While some view Eden's logic as nihilistic and depressing, this framing couldn't be further from how she understands her own perspective.

"If I thought that things weren't going to work out for me personally, *that* would be depressing," Eden says. "What I'm saying is we're all gonna fucking die. I mean, am I wrong?"

And the experts back her up.

"Have you heard of this 2030 spike theory?" says economist Roger T. Blarney. "Eden was telling me about it; basically, there's some smart people who think shit's really going to hit the fan in 2030. That's got me thinking I ought to retire! This job sucks, anyway."

However, Eden is still faced with her fair share of detractors.

"The apocalypse will be slow, and like all crises, it will impact the most marginalized groups first and most heavily," says climate activist Tia Lennox. "So I would say extinction isn't really a stable thing to bank on as a retirement plan. But then again, I'm a climate activist, and this girl's finances aren't really any of my concern, so she can do whatever she wants."

Eden has her hopes set on a hyper-specific end to humanity that will rid *everyone* of the need to keep a rainy-day fund.

"I don't hope to survive the end of times," Eden adds. "That sounds like more work than regular retirement. I'm just ready for the big one to really take us out so I can keep buying the occasional latte without feeling guilty, and so that the Earth can rebuild in the era that follows the end of human-wrought destruction."

Practical *and* socially conscious!

"I just hope the world doesn't end before we get the final season of *Succession*," Eden says. "But after that, I'm pretty much good to go!"

8 Things Other Than Your Productivity to Base Your Worth On:

- Hair shininess

- Easily calculating a 20 percent tip

- Compliments from others about your productivity

- Attention span (ability to watch seven-plus hours of television without drinking water)

- That time you made salmon

- The innate sanctity of being a living being (lol kidding)

- All those times you didn't make salmon (saving the salmon)

- Your ability to look at a big jar full of jelly beans and accurately guess how many jelly beans are in there

Conclusion:

Congrats, You Completed a Book!

Congrats! You've reached the end of this book! We're very proud of you for doing one simple thing *just for you*. Do you remember the excitement you felt when you cracked it open? Or the disappointment you felt when you thought a chapter was gonna end, but there were actually, like, seven pages left? That was our fault and we're sorry.

You might still be left wondering, "But how *do* I stay productive even though the world really feels like it has reached its *denouement*?" Well, there's no easy way to say this, but you purchased a satirical book of essays about how the double-bind of our need to work in order to have safety, security, and predictability is making us powerless in an increasingly unsafe, insecure, and unpredictable world. If your ultimate and sincere goal was to be more productive, we're happy for you but also deeply worried about you. Please, our office therapist has openings but she doesn't take insurance and she is NOT sliding scale.

The question we're really asking is *why* do we feel the need to be so ruthlessly productive all the time? Which parts of productivity culture are actually enriching our lives, and which parts feel like unspoken rules made up by some random guy who eats beef liver exclusively and wants you to do it, too? What other ways do we make meaning in our lives that are really just making us miserable and exhausted?

While we can and should work toward making the world a better, more livable, and more equitable place, it can all feel impossible given the scale of the problems at hand. But literally *every* aspect of capitalism is designed to make us feel as though we are not enough, and it will sell us anything that might make us feel happy for a brief moment at the cost of our own health and general wellbeing. The more this system keeps us feeling sad, isolated, and hopeless, the more it succeeds. It would be so much easier if a bath and one (1) edible could fix it all, but unfortunately and most ironically, happiness and progress under capitalism takes work. The primary work is fighting back against what is marketed to you, including the idea that your work defines you. Once you let these toxic ideas go, you will have more time to devote yourself to living a meaningful life. And that's why we hope that you can take a moment to reflect on these ideas and fundamentally change who you are to keep the world from burning.

Anyway, here are some photos of us putting in some long and painful hours writing this critique of capitalism and productivity culture in exchange for loads of money:

Here's Damien working through his third bout of COVID. Get 'em tiger!

Here's Sarah working on some edits during the birth of their first child. Aww!

Wow! Another Sunday in the office?

Looks like somebody's getting stress hives finishing this chapter!

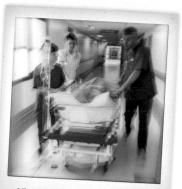

Uh-oh! Damien got hospitalized for "exhaustion" again!

Sarah takes up the practice of "microsleeping." Coworkers often think they have died.

Damien slurping porridge out of a CamelBak so he doesn't have to break for lunch. This was also his birthday!

Sarah skipping their best friends' wedding. We're all gonna laugh about this someday!

Firing our intern because she needed a "mental health day." Can't bullshit a bullshitter!

Trying to think of more jokes about work/life balance at 2 a.m. Hope it was worth it!

Acknowledgments

Thank you to our eternally patient agent, Abby Walters, and our incredible writers and models for this book: Sumayya Bisseret-Martinez, Kevin Burke, Justine Chung, Janine Cunningham, Madison Dillard, Alyson D'Lando, Ellena Eshraghi, Brandon Follick, McKayley Gourley, Heven Haile, Sio Hornbuckle, Julie Lim, Lizzie Logan, Andrew Martin, Ingrid Ostby, Seth Rubin, Freddie Shanel, Mai Tran, and Mara Wilson.

Thank you to Tricia Hersey, whose scholarship and activism dismantles grind culture while providing both a historical framework and a call to action, and whose philosophy was instrumental in undergirding the ethos of this work. And thank you to all of the organizers, artists, scholars, and workers who have been fighting for centuries to create a world where we all might feel a bit more human. We hope they keep doing this, and we'll keep writing jokes about it (till the Big One hits, or we get invited to be jesters on colonized Mars).

And to every boss who has ever Slacked us at midnight on a Sunday: Thank you for the inspiration.

About the Authors

The first and only satirical women's magazine, **Reductress** takes on the outdated perspectives and condescending tone of popular women's media. **Sarah Pappalardo** is the co-founder and editor of *Reductress*. **Damien Kronfeld** is the deputy editor of *Reductress*. Their previous book is *How to Win at Feminism: The Definitive Guide to Having It All—And Then Some!*

Andrews McMeel Publishing
a division of Andrews McMeel Universal
1130 Walnut Street, Kansas City, Missouri 64106

www.andrewsmcmeel.com

23 24 25 26 27 TEN 10 9 8 7 6 5 4 3 2 1

ISBN: 978-1-5248-7647-0

Library of Congress Control Number: 2022949707

Steve Jobs, Page 51, Photograph by Matthew Yohe (Wikicommons)
Bill Gates, Page 54, Photograph by Masaru Kamikura (Wikicommons)
Eleanor Roosevelt, Page 55, Photograph by Unknown (Wikicommons)
Happy Woman, Page 62, Photograph by "Boom" (Pexels)
Robot, Page 64, Photograph by Vincent Diamante (Wikicommons)
Kylie Jenner, Page 66, Photograph by Hayi (Wikicommons)
Person in suit looking contemplative, Page 68, Photograph by Zainul Febrian (Pexels)
Person on top of a mountain, Page 72, Photograph by Orlando Vera (Pexels)
Woman talking to doctor, Page 123, Photograph by Rodnae Productions (Pexels)
Man playing with niece, Page 94, Photograph by Gustavo Fring (Pexels)
Boomer Dad, Pages 20, 24, 29, 32, 34, 35, 37, 40, Photograph by Kaboompics (Pexels)

Editor: Charlie Upchurch
Art Director/Designer: Julie Barnes
Production Editor: Meg Utz
Production Manager: Shona Burns

ATTENTION: SCHOOLS AND BUSINESSES
Andrews McMeel books are available at quantity discounts with bulk purchase for educational, business, or sales promotional use. For information, please e-mail the Andrews McMeel Publishing Special Sales Department: sales@amuniversal.com.